THE CASTLE LECTURES IN ETHICS, POLITICS, AND ECONOMICS

The Culture
of the
New Capitalism

RICHARD SENNETT

Yale University Press   New Haven & London

Designed by James J. Johnson and set in Linotype Walbaum Roman
type by Integrated Publishing Solutions.

Printed in the United States of America.

The Library of Congress has cataloged the hardcover edition as follows:
Sennett, Richard, 1943–
    The culture of the new capitalism / Richard Sennett.
       p.   cm. — (The Castle lectures in ethics, politics, and economics)
    "This book was given as the Castle Lectures in Ethics, Politics, and
Economics, delivered by Richard Sennett at Yale University in 2004"—
T.p. verso.
    Includes bibliographical references and index.
    ISBN-13: 978-0-300-10782-1 (alk. paper)
    1. Industrial sociology. 2. Capitalism—Social aspects. 3. Industrial
organization. 4. Bureaucracy. 5. Economic history. I. Title. II. Series.
    HD6955.S46 2006
    306.3′6—dc22   2005014363

A catalogue record for this book is available from the British Library.

This paper meets the requirements of ANSI/NISO Z39.48-1992
(Permanence of Paper).

    ISBN-13: 978-0-300-11992-3 (pbk. : alk. paper)

10 9 8 7 6 5

This book was given as the
Castle Lectures in Ethics, Politics, and Economics,
delivered by Richard Sennett at
Yale University in 2004.

The Castle Lectures were endowed by John K. Castle. They honor his ancestor the Reverend James Pierpont, one of Yale's original founders. Given by established public figures, Castle Lectures are intended to promote reflection on the moral foundations of society and government and to enhance understanding of ethical issues facing individuals in our complex modern society.

Contents

Acknowledgments

A few years ago Yale University asked me to pull together the research and writing about labor which I'd done over the years. They made it sound simple: just provide an overview, in three of Yale's Castle Lectures. I should have known better; the task proved anything but simple and about much more than work.

I'd like to thank John Kulka of Yale University Press and especially Monika Krause, my research assistant, for helping me respond.

Introduction

Half a century ago, in the 1960s—that fabled era of free sex and free access to drugs—serious young radicals took aim at institutions, in particular big corporations and big government, whose size, complexity, and rigidity seemed to hold individuals in an iron grip. The Port Huron Statement, a founding document of the New Left in 1962, was equally hard on state socialism and multinational corporations; both regimes seemed bureaucratic prisons.

History has partly granted the framers of the Port Huron Statement their wish. The socialist rule of five-year plans, of centralized economic control, is gone. So is the capitalist corporation that provided employees jobs for life, that supplied the same products and services year after year. So also welfare institutions like health care and education have become less fixed in form and smaller in scale. The goal for rulers today, as for radicals fifty years ago, is to take apart rigid bureaucracy.

Yet history has granted the New Left its wish in a perverse form. The insurgents of my youth believed that by dismantling institutions they could produce communities: face-to-face relations of trust and solidarity, relations constantly negotiated and renewed, a communal realm in which people became sensitive to one another's needs. This certainly has not happened. The fragmenting of big institutions has left many people's lives in a fragmented state: the places they work more resembling train stations than villages, as family life is disoriented by the demands of work. Migration is the icon of the global age, moving on rather than settling in. Taking institutions apart has not produced more community.

If you are nostalgically minded—and what sensitive soul isn't?—you would find this state of affairs just one more reason for regret. Yet the past half century has been a time of unprecedented wealth creation, in

Asia and Latin America as well as in the global North, a generation of new wealth deeply tied to the dismantling of fixed government and corporate bureaucracies. So too has the technological revolution in the last generation flourished most in those institutions which are the least centrally controlled. Certainly such growth comes at a high price: ever greater economic inequality as well as social instability. Still, it would be irrational to believe that this economic explosion should never have happened.

Here is where culture enters the picture. I mean "culture" in its anthropological rather than artistic sense. What values and practices can hold people together as the institutions in which they live fragment? My generation suffered from a want of imagination in answering this question, in advancing the virtues of small-scale community. Community is not the only way to glue together a culture; most obviously, strangers in a city inhabit a common culture, even though they do not know one another. But the problem of a supportive culture is more than a matter of size.

Only a certain kind of human being can prosper in unstable, fragmentary social conditions. This ideal man or woman has to address three challenges.

The first concerns time: how to manage short-term relationships, and oneself, while migrating from task to task, job to job, place to place. If institutions no longer provide a long-term frame, the individual may have to improvise his or her life-narrative, or even do without any sustained sense of self.

The second challenge concerns talent: how to develop new skills, how to mine potential abilities, as reality's demands shift. Practically, in the modern economy, the shelf life of many skills is short; in technology and the sciences, as in advanced forms of manufacturing, workers now need to retrain on average every eight to twelve years. Talent is also a matter of culture. The emerging social order militates against the ideal of craftsmanship, that is, learning to do just one thing really well; such commitment can often prove economically destructive. In place of craftsmanship, modern culture advances an idea of meritocracy which celebrates potential ability rather than past achievement.

The third challenge follows from this. It concerns surrender; that is, how to let go of the past. The head of a dynamic company recently asserted that no one owns their place in her organization, that past service in particular earns no employee a guaranteed place. How could one respond to that assertion positively? A peculiar trait of personality is needed to do so, one which discounts the experiences a human being has already had. This trait of personality resembles more the consumer ever avid for new things, discarding old if perfectly serviceable goods, rather than the owner who jealousy guards what he or she already possesses.

What I want to show is how society goes about searching for this ideal man or woman. And I'll step beyond the scholar's remit in judging that search. A self oriented to the short term, focused on potential ability, willing to abandon past experience is—to put a kindly face on the matter—an unusual sort of human being. Most people are not like this; they need a sustaining life narrative, they take pride in being good at something specific, and they value the experiences they've lived through. The cultural ideal required in new institutions thus damages many of the people who inhabit them.

• • •

I need to tell the reader something about the kind of research experience I've had which leads me to this judgment. The New Left critique of big bureaucracy was my own, until in the late 1960s I began interviewing white, working-class families in Boston, people who were mostly second- or third-generation immigrants to the city. (The book Jonathan Cobb and I wrote about them is *The Hidden Injuries of Class*.) Far from being oppressed by bureaucracy, these were people anchored in solid institutional realities. Stable unions, big corporations, relatively fixed markets oriented them; within this frame, working-class men and women tried to make sense of their low status in a country supposedly making few class distinctions.

After this study, I left the subject of work for a while. It seemed that big American capitalism had achieved a triumphant plateau and that on this plane working-class life would continue in its fixed grooves. I could hardly have been more mistaken. The breakdown of the Bretton Woods currency agreements, after the oil crisis of 1973, meant national constraints on investing weakened; in turn that corporations reconfigured themselves to meet a new international clientele of investors—investors more intent on short-term profits in share prices than on long-term profits in dividends. Jobs began similarly and quickly to cross borders. So did consumption and communications. By the 1990s, thanks to microprocessing advances in electronics, the old dream/nightmare of automation began to become a reality in both manual and bureaucratic labor: at last it would be cheaper to invest in machines than to pay people to work.

So I returned to interviewing workers, though not now manual laborers but more middle-class workers who were at the epicenter of the global boom in high-tech industries, in financial services, and in the media. (This is the subject of my book *The Corrosion of Character.*) Here I had the chance to see the cultural ideal of the new capitalism at its most robust, the boom suggesting that this new man/woman would get rich by thinking short term, developing his or her potential, and regretting nothing. What I found instead were a large group of middle-class individuals who felt that their lives were cast adrift.

At the end of the 1990s the boom began to go bust, as is normally the case in any business cycle. As the economy sobered up, however, it became evident that the global growth spurt had left an enduring trace on non-business institutions, particularly institutions of the welfare state. This stamp is as much cultural as structural. The values of the new economy have become a reference point for how government thinks about dependence and self-management in health care and pensions, or again about the kind of skills the education system provides. Since I'd grown up "on welfare," as the American phrase has it, the new cultural model formed for me a vivid contrast to the culture of the housing project in Chicago where I spent my childhood. (This stamp is the subject of my book *Respect in an Age of Inequality*.)

I've sought to avoid in this book simply summarizing what I've written before. In my earlier writings, I neglected the role of consumption in the new economy; here I try, briefly, to address how new forms of consumption diminish possessiveness, and the political consequences which follow. I've had to think harder than in the past about the relation of power and authority in work. Looking backward has prompted me to look forward, to begin exploring the spirit of craftsmanship in mental as well as manual labor.

Most of all, I've had to rethink the Americanness of the research I've done. In the 1970s, America dominated the world's economy, and in the 1990s, even if people around the globe were involved in the process, the United States led the institutional changes which produced a new kind of economy. American researchers thus easily imagine that they can substitute interchangeably the words *American* and *modern*. This fantasy is no longer possible. The Chinese road to growth is quite different from that of the United States, and more powerful. The economy of the European Union is larger than that of America and also in some respects more efficient, even in its new member states, again without mimicking America.

Foreign readers of my recent books have tended to view them as providing reasons to reject an American way of working which other places would follow at their peril. This is not quite what I intend. Certainly the structural changes I describe lack national boundaries; the decline of lifetime employment, for instance, is not an American phenomenon. What is "culture-bound" is the particular ways in which Americans understand the changes which have come over material life.

A stereotype holds that Americans are aggressive competitors in business. Beneath this stereotype lies a different, more passive mentality. Americans of the middling sort I've interviewed in the past decade have tended to accept structural change with resignation, as though the loss of security at work and in schools run like businesses are inevitable: you can do little about such basic shifts, even if they hurt you. The dismantling of large institutions which I describe is, however, not a divine commandment. Nor, indeed, is it yet the norm in American work; the new economy is still only a small part of the whole economy. It does exert a profound moral and normative force as a cutting-edge standard for how the larger economy should evolve. My hope is that Americans will in time treat this economy as outsiders tend to see it: a proposition for change which, like any proposition, should be subject to rigorous critique.

•   •   •

In this regard, the reader should be aware of the critical mind-set of ethnographers. We spend hours listening to people, alone or in groups, explain themselves, their values, their fears, and their hopes. As the hours unfold, all these matters are reformatted and revised in the act of telling. The alert ethnographer pays attention to what causes people to contradict themselves or, equally, why people arrive at a dead end in understanding. The interviewer is not hearing a faulty report, but rather listening to a subjective investigation of social complexity. Such ambiguities, deformations, and difficulties which appear in personally accounting Faith, the Nation, or Class constitute an individual's understanding of culture.

This sociological craft is both eminently suited and unsuited to uncovering the sense of innovation today. Suited, because society's emphasis on flow and flux intersects with the process of working through an interpretation in one's mind. Unsuited, because most subjects participate in in-depth interviews in order to reach conclusions, to arrive at an explanation of how they are placed in the world. Fluidity frustrates this desire; ideological proposals for how to prosper in "the new" prove elusive, once people ponder them long enough.

In responding to Yale's invitation to describe the culture of the new capitalism, I've thus had to think about the limitations of my particular craft and about the frustrations of subjective investigation. I've taken, therefore, the great and unpardonable liberty of speaking for the people I've interviewed over the years; I've tried to summarize what's in their minds. In taking this liberty, I am aware of sweeping under the carpet perhaps the most basic cultural problem: much of modern social reality is illegible to the people trying to make sense of it.

The chapters that follow treat three subjects: how institutions are changing; how fears about being made redundant or left behind are related to talent in the "skills society"; how consumption behavior relates to political attitudes. The institutional changes I describe in the workplace in fact refer to only the cutting edge of the economy: high technology, global finance, and new service firms with three thousand or more employees. Most people in North America and Western Europe do not work for such firms. Yet this small slice of the economy has a cultural influence far beyond its numbers. These new institutions suggest the new formulation of personal skills and abilities; the combined formula of institution and ability shapes the culture of consumption; consumption behavior in turn influences politics, particularly progressive politics. I am unabashedly inferring the culture of the whole from a small part of society, just because the avatars of a particular kind of capitalism have persuaded so many people that their way is the way of the future.

The apostles of the new capitalism argue that their version of these three subjects—work, talent, consumption—adds up to more freedom in modern society, a fluid freedom, a "liquid modernity" in the apt phrase of the philosopher Zygmunt Bauman.[1] My quarrel with them is not whether their version of the new is real; institutions, skills, and consumption patterns have indeed changed. My argument is that these changes have not set people free.

CHAPTER ONE

Bureaucracy

The Fresh Page of the Present

We best begin by giving some substance to the contrast between new and old, and at the very outset we are caught up short. "All that is solid melts into air," Karl Marx famously wrote about capitalism—one hundred and sixty years ago.[1] His version of "liquid modernity" came from an idealized past. In part it reflected nostalgia for the age-old rhythms of the countryside, which Marx never knew firsthand. Similarly, he regretted the demise of premodern craft guilds and the settled life of burghers in cities, both of which would have spelled death to his own revolutionary project.

Instability since Marx's day may seem capitalism's only constant. The upheavals of markets, the fast dancing of investors, the sudden rise, collapse, and movement of factories, the mass migration of workers seeking better jobs or any job: such images of capitalism's energy pervaded the nineteenth century and were conjured at the beginning of the last century in another famous phrase, this by the sociologist Joseph Schumpeter: "creative destruction."[2] Today the modern economy seems full of just this unstable energy, due to the global spread of production, markets, and finance and to the rise of new technologies. Yet today those involved in making change argue that we are not plunged into more turmoil, but rather are on a fresh page of history.

Black-and-white contrasts are always suspect, especially when they suggest progress. Take the issue of inequality. In Britain, just before the agricultural crisis of the 1880s, four thousand families owned 43 percent of the nation's wealth. In the last two decades of the twentieth century, inequality was different in context but equally pronounced. In both Britain and America, the wealth of the top fifth of families grew during these decades, the top tenth grew greatly, and the top

1 percent grew exponentially. Though immigrants at the bottom also gained wealth, incomes of the middle three-fifths of the Anglo-American population have stagnated. A recent study by the International Labor Organization refines this picture of inequality: as income inequality increased during the 1990s, the loss of wealth share was markedly acute among part-time and under-employed workers. Increasing inequality also marks the elderly population, across the British–American spectrum.[3]

Another misleading feature of this black-and-white contrast is to assume that stable societies are economically stagnant. This wasn't the case in Germany before the First World War or in America after the Second World War, and it's not the case today—in smaller economies like those of Norway and Sweden. Despite the Nordic tendency to gloomy introspection, the northern European rim managed to combine relative stability with growth and has preserved a more equitable distribution of wealth and a generally higher standard of quality of life than America and Britain.

Perhaps the most debatable "new" is globalization. The sociologist Leslie Sklair has argued, with a wealth of economic detail, that globalization has simply expanded the multinational corporation of the mid–twentieth century.[4] His view is that the Chinese may eventually assume the role American multinationals once played, but the game is still the same. Against him, his fresh-page critics marshall another host of indubitable material facts: the rise of immense cities linked in a global economy all their own; innovations in communications technology and in transport which little resemble where people used to live, how they made contact with others, or how goods once traveled.

This debate is about more than economic circumstances. The multinational corporation used to be intertwined with the politics of the nation-state. Today, proponents of the fresh-page thesis argue, the global corporation has investors and shareholders throughout the world and a structure of ownership too complex to serve single national interests—the petroleum giant Shell, for instance, has cut free from both Dutch and British political constraints. The most radical case for the uniqueness of our times would be that nations are losing their economic value.

I want to focus on a then-and-now issue which is perhaps less familiar. This is an argument about institutions.

The fresh-page proposition assumes that Marx got the history of capitalism wrong. (The word *capitalism* itself was a later construction of the sociologist Werner Sombart.) Marx erred precisely by believing in constant creative destruction. In the view of his critics, the capitalist system soon ossified into a hardened shell; at first the routines of the factory combined with the anarchy of stock markets, but by the end of the nineteenth century, anarchy had subsided and the hardened shell of bureaucracy in corporations had become even thicker. Only today has that shell been cracked apart. There's a good measure of factual truth in this view of the past, but not quite on the terms laid out by enthusiasts of the fresh page.

The factories of the early nineteenth century certainly combined mind-numbing routine with unstable employment; not only did workers lack protective clout, but the businesses themselves were often poorly structured and so liable to sudden collapse. By one estimate, 4 percent of able-bodied workers were unemployed in London in 1850; the rate of new-business failure topped 70 percent. Most firms in the 1850s did not publish the facts of their operation, if indeed they had gathered them, and accounting procedures tended to simple statements of profit and loss. The operation of the business cycle was not understood statistically until the end of the nineteenth century. These were the kinds of data Marx had in mind when describing the industrial order's material and mental instability.

But this "primitive" capitalism was indeed too primitive to survive socially and politically; primitive capitalism was a recipe for revolution. Over a hundred-year stretch, from the 1860s through the 1970s, corporations learned the art of stability, assuring the longevity of businesses and increasing the number of employed. The free market did not effect this stabilizing change; rather, the way businesses were internally organized played a more significant role. They were saved from revolution by applying military models of organization to capitalism.

It's to Max Weber that we owe the analysis of the militarization of civil society at the end of the nineteenth century—corporations operating increasingly like armies in which everyone had a place and each place a defined function.[5]

As a young man Weber witnessed with mixed emotions the growth of a new, united Germany. The Prussian army had for centuries a legendary reputation

for efficiency. Whereas many European armies continued to sell places for officers, no matter their ability,
and to give ordinary soldiers primitive training, the
Prussian military emphasized getting things right. Its
chain of command was tighter than those of its French
and British counterparts; it defined with more logical
rigor the duties of each rank in the chain of command.
In Otto von Bismarck's Germany this military model
began to be applied to businesses and to the institutions
of civil society, principally, in Bismarck's mind, for the
sake of peace and the prevention of revolution. No
matter how poor he may be, the worker who knows he
has an established position is less likely to revolt than
the worker who can't make any sense of his or her position in society. This was the founding politics of what
can be called social capitalism.

Ironically, Schumpeter's own early analyses of the
economy showed that as this militarized, social capitalism spread, business turned a profit. This was so because while the thirst for a quick dollar, pound, or franc
remained, investors also hungered for more predictable, long-term yields. At the end of the nineteenth
century, the language of investment decisions first took
on a military cast—one which invoked investment

campaigns and strategic thinking and, the pet idea of General Carl von Clausewitz, outcome analysis—for good reason. Sudden profits had proved illusive, particularly in infrastructure projects like railroad and urban transport construction. In the twentieth century, workers joined the process of strategic planning; their building societies and unions aimed equally at stabilizing and guaranteeing the position of workers.

The profits that markets put in jeopardy, bureaucracy sought to repair. Bureaucracy seemed more *efficient* than markets. This "search for order," as the historian Robert Wiebe called it, spread from business into government and then into civil society. When the lesson of strategic profit passed into the ideals about effective government, the status of civil servants rose; their bureaucratic practices were ever more insulated from swings in politics.[6] In civil society proper, schools became increasingly standardized in operation and in content; professions brought order to the practices of medicine, law, and science. For Weber, all these forms of rationalizing institutional life, coming originally from a military source, would lead to a society whose norms of fraternity, authority, and aggression were equally military in character, though civilian people might not be aware they thought like soldiers. As a general observer of modern times, Weber feared a twentieth century dominated by the ethos of armed struggle. As a political economist, Weber argued specifically that the army is a more consequent model for modernity than the market.

Time lay at the center of this military, social capitalism: long-term and incremental and above all predictable time. This bureaucratic imposition affected individuals as much as institutional regulations. Rationalized time enabled people to think about their lives as narratives—narratives not so much of what necessarily will happen as of how things should happen. It became possible, for instance, to define what the stages of a career ought to be like, to correlate long-term service in a firm to specific steps of increased wealth. Many manual workers could for the first time plan how to buy a house. The reality of business upheavals and opportunities prevented such strategic thinking. In the flux of the real world, particularly in the flux of the business cycle, reality did not of course proceed according to plan, but now the idea of being able to plan defined the realm of individual agency and power.

Rationalized time cut deep into subjective life. The German word *Bildung* names a process of personal formation which fits a young person for the lifelong conduct of life. If in the nineteenth century Bildung acquired an institutional frame, in the twentieth century, the results became concrete, displayed at midcentury in works like William Whyte's *The Organization Man*, C. Wright Mills's *White Collar*, and Michel Crozier's *Bureaucracy*. Whyte's view of bureaucratic Bildung is that steadiness of purpose becomes more important than sudden bursts of ambition within the organization, which bring only short-term rewards. Crozier's analysis of Bildung in French corporations dwelt on the ladder as an imaginative object, organizing the individual's understanding of himself; one climbs up or down or remains stationary, but there is always a rung on which to step.

The fresh-page thesis asserts that the institutions which enabled this life-narrative thinking have now "melted into air." The militarization of social time is coming apart. There are some obvious institutional facts on which this thesis is founded. The end of lifetime employment is one such, as is the waning of careers spent within a single institution; so is the fact, in the public realm, that government welfare and safety nets have become more short-term and more erratic. The financial guru George Soros encapsulates such changes by saying that "transactions" have replaced "relationships" in people's dealings with one another.[7] The immense growth of the world economy is cited by others as possible only because institutional controls on the flow of goods, services, and labor have become less coherent; these have enabled an unprecedented number of migrants to inhabit the so-called gray economies of large cities. The collapse of the Soviet Empire in 1989 is cited by others as putting paid to an institutional order in which military regulation and civil society were indistinguishable.

This debate about institutionalized time is as much about culture as about economics and politics. It turns on Bildung. Perhaps I can suggest how by recourse to my own research experience.

When I began interviewing software programmers in Silicon Valley in the early 1990s, they seemed to be drunk on the possibilities of technology as well as on the prospect of sudden wealth. Many of these young programmers, in emulation of Bill Gates at Microsoft, had dropped out of university careers to write software.

Their anonymous offices south of San Francisco stank of stale pizzas; futons and sleeping bags lined the floors. They felt at the edge of a momentous shift: none of the old rules, I was told frequently, now applied. Investors in their projects also seemed to think so; companies with no earning shot up overnight in value and as quickly plummeted; the bankers moved on. The young techies had a mind-set completely at odds with that of the young bureaucrats depicted in the pages of Whyte and Crozier. They despised steadiness of purpose, and when they failed, as they often did, like the bankers they simply moved on. Their tolerance of failure most impressed me: it seemed to have no personal implication for them.

When the dot-com bubble burst in 2000 and Silicon Valley began to be ruled by prudence these young people discovered the reality of living on a fresh page. The most common reaction I heard was that the young programmers felt suddenly alone. "No one wants to know you anymore," one told me; "they've heard too many bright ideas before." "The 'scene' has moved to Boston," another said, "to biotech-land, and I don't belong there." Alone, they suddenly discovered time— the shapeless time which had before exhilarated them, the absence of rules for how to proceed, how to move ahead. Their fresh page was blank. In this limbo, isolated, without a life narrative, they discovered failure.

It could be said that this discovery is not too different from that of the machinist whose craft has disappeared; or in another way of the student tempted by a course in media studies, knowing that millions of other young people are similarly tempted. They all face the prospect of drift.

It is against that prospect of drifting in isolation that we ought frame the cultural difference between new and old; the cultural divide takes us deeper into the life of institutions.

Social Capitalism

Max Weber at one and the same time analyzed, admired, and feared a domestic solution to social order based on military form. As an analyst, he realized that the Prussian model would set capitalism on a different course than that predicted by Marx—but what exactly would life be like inside? Just as a well-run army is designed to survive defeats on the battlefield, a well-run business had to be designed to survive market booms and busts. Beyond Germany's borders, Weber saw the evidence for this proposition: the powerful vertical trusts and monopolies in the United States suppressed market competition; their owners, like Andrew Carnegie and John D. Rockefeller, behaved like domestic generals.

The genius of this system lay specifically in how the chain of command was organized. Since the days of Adam Smith, managers had a clear idea of how the division of labor worked. The Smithian model explored how a complex task had to be broken up into parts in order to produce efficiently a carriage or a cheese. The measure of efficiency crudely lay in how much of a thing could be produced quickly, but the real test of Smithian production came in the marketplace—could you more quickly than your competitors produce lots of things other people wanted to buy? While armies operate through the division of labor, Weber realized that competition and efficiency take on a different character in military life.

On the battlefield some soldiers are going to lose everything, and those soldiers have to be willing to obey even if they know they are doomed to die. The social compact in armies, among soldiers, has to be absolute. For an army to hold together, the functions of each rank need to be clear and precise, no matter who is alive to perform them, no matter whether the army is winning or losing. This military necessity informed Weber's analysis of bureaucratic "office" in domestic life—the term *office* he applies to everyone from the janitor to the president of a large bureaucracy.

As in an army, so in a big domestic bureaucracy, effective power is shaped like a pyramid. The pyramid is "rationalized," that is, each office, each part, has a defined function. As you move up the chain of command there should be ever fewer people in control; conversely, as you move down, the less powerful people are, the more the organization can include. You are good at your job by doing that job and no other. In the liberal, Smith model, you prosper by doing more than expected; in the military, Weberian model you are punished for stepping out of line.

Time is of the essence to this Weberian model: the functions are fixed, static. They have to be, so that the organization holds together, no matter who occupies any particular office. And yet if the structure is designed to survive the upheavals of events, the Weberian pyramid has a historic resonance.

Weber was struck by the social compact which Bismarck sought to forge with German workers; the chancellor and his ministers promised everyone a place in the social system. The pyramid shape enables this promise: it permits a corporation to add ever more people at the lower ranks, just as an army can absorb ever more foot soldiers. Put fancifully, structures of this sort can become obese for the sake of social inclusion——as evident in our own day in Italian and Indian bureaucracies. Bismarck's hardheaded reason for fattening up institutions was pacification——the avoidance of strife by giving everyone a place. The political and social rational of fat bureaucracy is thus inclusion rather than efficiency.

Weber partly admired this militarization of domestic institutions just for that reason——he was no friend of revolution. And he saw in the pyramid a certain further social justice: each office defines the talents and skills a person needs for inclusion, the obligations he or she has to fulfill; in this sense, the bureaucracy is transparent. But he was also deeply unhappy about the personal consequences which bureaucratic stability and transparency entail.

At the end of his most renowned essay, *The Protestant Ethic and the Spirit of Capitalism*, that unhappiness jumps off the page. The person who makes a life career in such an institution lives in an "iron cage."[8] Or, to use another analogy, the lived time in a fixed-function organization is like slowly crawling up, or down, the stairs in a house you have not designed; you are living some-one else's design for your life. In the *Protestant Ethic,* Weber explains specifically why a person would do so: bureaucracies teach the discipline of delayed gratification. Instead of judging whether your immediate activities matter to you, you learn to think about a future reward which will come if you obey orders now. And just here there opens up a gap between the military and the domestic pyramid.

Militarism does offer immediate gratification—service to one's country and solidarity with one's fellow soldiers. Whereas, in Weber's view, the future gratifications and fulfillments promised in domestic bureaucracies often never arrive. He gives this frustration a subjective twist; a person who has learned the discipline of delay often cannot permit himself to arrive. Many driven individuals harbor this perverse sentiment. They feel whatever they have is not good enough, and they are incapable of enjoying the present for its own sake; delay of fulfillment becomes a way of life. Weber's insight was to give the subjective impulse an institutional context. Climbing the steps of the bureaucracy can become a way of life. If the iron cage is a prison, it can thus also become a psychological home.

•   •   •

The Weberian pyramid became a structural reality, dominating large organizations in the twentieth century, but not quite psychologically on Weber's terms. Giant manufacturing plants like General Motors' Willow Run auto factory became pyramids, the entire manufacturing process gathered within a single building the size of a small town: raw materials went in one door, as it were, and a finished automobile drove out the door at the opposite end. The pyramid unified, centralized, concentrated. In such big factories and in their office peers, the division of labor was initially pursued on Adam Smith's terms, Frederick Taylor and other efficiency experts seeking to micromanage every movement and every moment of an employee's labor. These efforts to mechanize human beings modulated to Weber's terrain, both employers and unions seeking to stabilize and regularize these institutional monsters even if it meant sacrificing efficiency.

The welfare state also assumed the form of a bureaucratic pyramid. In social-democratic principle, welfare benefits, like old-age pensions and education, were conceived as universal rights; in practice, even Nordic and British welfare systems obliged their clients to think like bureaucrats in dealing with their own needs. The bureaucratic rules served the bureaucracy first and foremost; elderly, students, the unemployed, and the sick were obliged to behave like officeholders in the Weberian sense rather than as individuals with distinctive life histories. The system focused ever more on institutional self-maintenance and stability rather than on the effective delivery of care.

It cannot surprise the sociologist, in a way, that the first half of the twentieth century was devoted to war, for the organization of armies had become the very model for civil society. Yet the "militarization of society" carries false implications, were we to imagine that it produced a mass of blind, subservient, obedient workers or welfare clients. Had Weber more actual experience of military life he would have understood why.

In an army, orders modulate as they pass down a chain of command: what the general decrees, the military staff begins to translate into practice, adapting the command to conditions in the field; sergeants, corporals, and rank privates try in their turn to make sense of the command on a particular patch of ground. All obey, but equally, all interpret. When an order translates into action, the key word is "translates." The larger the army, the more interpretation is required.

The same mediation marks domestic pyramids and is one reason the apostles of efficiency like Taylor failed. His time-and-motion studies produced something like a field marshall's writ about what things should happen and how they were to be done. In practice, each of these precepts was interpreted and negotiated as it passed down the institutional structure. With a childlike innocence, Taylor fretted that his precepts—so clear, so "scientific"—became smudged and messed in the corporations for whom he consulted. Reality failed him.

The interpretative modulation built into any bureaucratic pyramid is one reason that, in my fieldwork for *The Corrosion of Character*, I encountered many people who did not conform to the psychology Weber set out for the domestic iron cage. For instance, workers for IBM, which before 1993 operated like a paternalistic army, certainly felt caged in by the corporation's self-maintaining structure. But within these confines they negotiated the concrete things they were told to do and interpreted the meaning, for them as individuals, of moving from one department to another.[9] The social analyst would dismiss at his or her peril these small translations. Performing them afforded people in the corporation a sense of their own agency; the institutional narrative of promotion and demotion became their own life story. As in armies so in corporations: unhappiness with an institution can coexist with strong commitment to it; a person, even if generally unhappy, who is given room to make sense of things on his or her own patch becomes bonded to the organization.

In my fieldwork for *Respect*, I found this combination of disaffection and commitment even stronger among public service workers in welfare-state, pyramidal bureaucracies. In Chicago and in London I spoke to teachers in poorly provisioned, sclerotic inner-city schools; in New York I interviewed nurses in the city's abysmal public hospitals. Many of them could have left for better jobs, but didn't. They spoke of doing something useful.[10] What more personally bound them were, again, those small steps of negotiation and mediation which established their personal presence in their institutions. A nurse in New York told me that this is why she stayed in an impoverished public hospital rather than did more lucrative work as a temporary nurse. Both ways of nursing are useful, but in the hospital she "made a difference."

If I had to make one firsthand conclusion about the structure that Bismarck devised for social capitalism, which Weber so brilliantly analyzed, I would say that its greatest legacy was the gift of organized time. All social relationships take time to develop; a life narrative in which the individual matters to others requires an institution with lifetime longevity. Certainly, driven individuals can waste their lives jockeying for position in such institutions. But most adults learn how to tame the beast of ambition; we live for more than that reason. Iron cages have framed the time of living with other people. More, bureaucratic structures provide the occasion for interpreting power, for making sense of it on the ground; they thus can give individuals a sense of agency. Even in dysfunctional institutions like those of the American welfare state, public service

workers will stay in the belief that they can make a difference. Is this an illusion? Perhaps, but no adult can
proceed without it.

Given its military origins, the image of the iron
cage suggests a bureaucracy built to survive upheaval.
We equate bureaucracy with stability and solidity. Yet
here is truly an illusion. Social capitalism has proved
fragile. Its bureaucratic structure, in our own generation, has been challenged in ways which neither Bismarck nor Weber could have predicted.

Uncaged

The late twentieth century turned three new pages
which seemed to suggest that social capitalism would
become a nostalgic memory. The economic changes are
internally complex; I will simplify by selecting those
aspects which have most directly affected ordinary
people's lives in institutions.

First has been the shift from managerial to shareholder power in large companies. This shift has a precise date: an enormous surplus of capital for investment
was unleashed on a global scale when the Bretton Woods

agreements broke down in the early 1970s. Wealth which had been confined to local or national enterprises or stored in national banks could much more easily move round the globe. Notably in the oil-rich countries of the Middle East, in American, Japanese, and German banks, and among the network of ethnic Chinese in the Pacific there was a hunger for investment. Giant pension funds and small private investors followed their lead in the 1980s and 1990s, searching for new, offshore opportunities.[11]

The banking business transformed itself to cope with this cornucopia. Merchant banking became truly international. In London, for instance, the networks forged by the old merchant bankers in Britain's imperial past were now appropriated by American, Japanese, and German banks, who bought out the British firms; today the City of London remains a site for global finance, but the City is no longer a British institution. The business banks did focused increasingly on mergers and acquisitions, and these too lost connection to nation-state interests. Siegmund Warburg had in the 1950s pioneered the techniques of hostile takeovers of large, nation-based companies. One consequence of the outpouring of wealth was that the hostile takeover became a form of art, as money looked for ever new ways to install itself.

Initially, managers thought they were dealing with investors familiar to them from the past, that is, largely passive institutions and individuals. The workings of a firm would be confirmed at annual meetings where the only challenges would come from oddly dressed elderly ladies or vegetarian activists. The managers were soon disabused. Investors became active judges; a turning point in such participation occurred when pension funds, controlling vast quantities of capital, began actively pressuring management. The increasing sophistication of financial instruments like the leveraged buyout meant that investors could make or break corporations while its management stood by helplessly.

Due to the emergence of sophisticated shareholder power, corporate generals at the top of the chain of command were not the generals they once were; a new source of lateral power had emerged at the top, often literally foreign, often otherwise indifferent, to the culture that long-term associations and alliances had forged within the corporation.

This shift in power turned a second new page. The empowered investors wanted short-term rather than long-term results. They formed the cadres of what Bennett Harrison calls "impatient capital." Importantly, share price rather than corporate dividends was their measure of results. Buying and selling shares in an open, fluid market yielded quicker—and greater— yields than holding stocks for the long term. For this reason, whereas in 1965 American pension funds held stocks on an average for 46 months, by 2000 much in the portfolios of these institutional investors turned over on an average of 3.8 months. The price trade in stock overturned traditional measures of performance like price/earnings ratios—famously in the technology boom of the 1990s, when share values soared in companies with no earnings.

Of course there's nothing new about money looking for a home or a quick dollar. But the combined effect of so much unleashed capital and the pressure of short-term returns transformed the structure of those institutions most attractive to empowered investors. Enormous pressure was put on companies to look beautiful in the eyes of the passing voyeur; institutional beauty consisted in demonstrating signs of internal change and flexibility, appearing to be a dynamic company, even if the once-stable company had worked perfectly well. Firms like Sunbeam and Enron became dysfunctional or corrupt in responding to this investor parade, but even in periods of market downturn the pressure on firms remained the same: institutional solidity become an investment negative rather than a positive. Stability seemed a sign of weakness, suggesting to the market that the firm could not innovate or find new opportunities or otherwise manage change.

Here was a profound contrast to both practice and theory in an earlier generation. Rockefeller reassured the markets by eliminating competition and flux; the social compact within Weber's model depended on the conviction of those within that the institution could weather any storm outside. Now the willingness to destabilize one's own organization sent a positive signal. Among chief executives, Louis Gerstner of IBM stands out in this regard, a man who in 1993 inherited the most rigid of iron cage bureaucracies and by 1996 had dismantled a great deal of what he had inherited.

At the outset of this chapter, I invoked the image of an ideal self willing to let go, to surrender possession. That ideal became a practical necessity for executives trying to cope with the pressures of impatient capital. They had to reengineer, reinvent themselves continually or falter in the markets.

The third challenge to the iron cage lay in the development of new technologies of communication and manufacturing. Communication on a global scale became instant. Some analysts, like Manuel Castells, imagine that the global economy left the ground and took to the skies, place no longer mattering; others, like Saskia Sassen, argue that big cities, where the work of investment and coordination gets done, became even more important in the global age. From the vantage point of people within institutions, the communications revolution had yet another meaning.

The growth of communications technology meant that information could be formulated in unambiguous and thorough terms, disseminated in its original version throughout a corporation. E-mail and its derivatives diminished the mediation and interpretation of commands and rules verbally passing down the chain of command. Thanks to new computer tools for mapping corporate inputs and outputs, information on how projects, sales, and personnel were performing could pass up to the top, instantly and unmediated. In the auto industry in the 1960s, the time lag of getting an

executive decision on to the shop floor was, by one estimate, five months, an interval that today has been dramatically cut to a few weeks. In sales organization, sales
reps' performances can be mapped in real time on
home-office computer screens.

One consequence of the information revolution
has thus been to replace modulation and interpretation
of commands by a new kind of centralization. The social implications of such centralization, as we shall
shortly see, run deep. For executives driven by impatient
capital, the immediate result of technological advance
was to prompt in them the belief that they knew enough
and so could command immediate change from the top.
That belief would often prove their undoing.

Automation, another side of the technological
revolution, has affected the bureaucratic pyramid in
one profound way: the base of an institution no longer
needs to be big. Both in manual and in white-collar
work, organizations can now efficiently shed routine
jobs thanks to such innovations as bar code readers,
voice recognition technologies, three-dimensional object scanners as well as the micromachines that do the
work of fingers. It's not just that the sheer size of the
workforce can be reduced, but also that savings can be

effected by management aiming to cut out the functional layers at the bottom—an institutional army in which the privates are circuits.

Such technological capacity means that inclusion of the masses—the social element of social capitalism—can wither. Just the most vulnerable members of society, those with the desire to work but without specialized human skills, are likely to be left out. Of course the industries and offices of an earlier era were not run as charities. As Bismarck was the first to recognize, however, business growth generates social dislocation and unrest, threats which can be addressed by spreading out the employment base. To create jobs for all in this old way now is to defy or ignore modern technological power.

As automation spreads, the field of fixed human skills shrinks. Fifty years ago, holding a conversation with a machine about one's bank account would have seemed a sci-fi fantasy; today it's taken for granted. Here again appears the idealized new self: an individual constantly learning new skills, changing his or her "knowledge basis." In reality that ideal is driven by the necessity of keeping ahead of the machine.

All three of the new pages I've described apply at present only to certain kinds of economic bureaucracies. They are big, they sell shares in themselves, and they can profit from advanced technology. Such firms are to be found in financial, legal, and insurance services and in global manufacturing and shipping; they draw on quite specialized smaller-scale services such as product design, advertising and marketing, media, and computer design.

By contrast, the majority of firms in America and Britain have fewer than three thousand employees; many have only a local reach or are family-owned; some are craft-services like the small-scale construction companies. These firms can function perfectly well as small bureaucratic pyramids. If you were an elderly investor, you'd sleep more soundly owning a local plumbing company than venturing into the derivatives market. And Weber remains a reliable guide to the inner workings of such small pyramid firms.

It's important to keep this in mind in evaluating the globalized, short-term value, technologically complex organization as a model of institutional change. Big governments and civic institutions have tried to dismantle their institutional past following this model.

The very image of large, stable bureaucracies providing long-term, predictable benefits horrifies political reformers. There is, of course, no equivalent in government coffers of the cash mountain on which modern global investors sit. Governments' "investors" are the workers who will eventually receive pensions and health care, the parents who pay taxes for schools—all inside stakeholders. Why should a business model attractive to a short-term Saudi oil magnate appeal to them?

Here culture again enters the picture, in the image of that idealized self which can prosper in the leveraged buyout world. This idealized person eschews dependency; he or she does not cling to others. Reformers of the welfare state fear it has encouraged institutionalized dependency—which is just what Bismarck hoped for. In place of life within the institution, reformers famously want more personal initiative and enterprise: vouchers for education, employee savings accounts for old age and for medical care, one's welfare conducted as a kind of consulting business.

It's misleading to equate the fear of dependency with individualism *tout court*. In the new-business world, those who prosper require a thick network of social contacts; one of the reasons global cities take form is precisely that they provide a local territory for face-to-face networking. People who are connected to organizations only by computer, working at home or selling out in the field on their own, tend to be marginalized, missing out on the informal contacts sometimes called the water cooler connection.

The fear of dependence names rather a worry about loss of self-control and, more psychologically, a feeling of shame in deferring to others. One of the great ironies of the new-economy model is that, in taking apart the iron cage, it has only succeeded in reinstituting these social and emotional traumas in a new institutional form.

Institutional Architecture

The new page of institutions is not a blank page. We might think about what's written on it by comparing the new institutional architecture to a uniquely modern machine rather than to a traditional building-type like the pyramid.

Specifically, this new structure performs like an MP3 player. The MP3 machine can be programmed to play only a few bands from its repertoire; similarly, the flexible organization can select and perform only a few of its many possible functions at any given time. In the old-style corporation, by contrast, production occurs via a fixed set of acts; the links in the chain are set. Again, in an MP3 player, what you hear can be programmed in any sequence. In a flexible organization, the sequence of production can also be varied at will. In high-tech software programming firms, for instance, the institution might focus on some promising, innovative bit of imaging work, then go back to build the routine code support which simplifies the imaging, then go forward to think through commercial possibilities. This is task-oriented rather than fixed-function labor. Linear development is replaced by a mind-set willing to jump around.

This new way of working permits what management-speak calls the delayering of institutions. By outsourcing some functions to other firms or other places, the manager can get rid of layers within the organization. The organization swells and contracts, employees are added and discarded as the firm moves from one task to another.

The "casualization" of the labor force refers to more than the use of outside temps or subcontractors;

it applies to the internal structure of the firm. Employees can be held to three- or six-month contracts, often renewed over the course of years; the employer can thereby avoid paying them benefits like health care or pensions. More, workers on short contracts can be easily moved from task to task, the contracts altered to suit the changing activities of the firm. And the firm can contract and expand quickly, shedding or adding personnel.

It's easier to quantify the numbers of temps than of short-term workers within firms, but the numbers are striking such as they are. Temporary labor is the fastest growing sector of the labor force in the United States and Britain; all found, temp-work accounts for 8 percent of the U.S. labor force today. If we add to this number people employed on a short-term, benefits-avoiding basis in retail sales, restaurants, and other service work, the percentage would climb to something like a fifth of the American labor force.

Taken together, these three building blocks of institutions—casualization, delayering, and nonlinear sequencing—shorten the organization's time frame; immediate and small tasks become the emphasis. The development of the commercial Internet was a marvel in this regard, a hugely complicated communications system developed quickly, in pieces. One of its attractions to investors was precisely the frenzy of movement, change, and chaos in firms, the more churning the more beckoning. Few investors knew what they were buying—save that it was new.

• • •

Socially, short-term task labor alters how workers work together. In the chain-of-command pyramid, you do your duty and fulfill your function, and eventually you are rewarded, as the holder of an office, for performance or seniority; or passed over or demoted. Either way, the infrastructure of the firm is clear enough. In shifting, short-term task-labor, it isn't. The structure of the firm is not a solid object to study, its future cannot be predicted. In interviewing temps, I've found that those who prosper in this milieu have a high tolerance for ambiguity. One administrative assistant told me, "Each time you start a new job, you need to fake it. The boss expects you know how things should be done and what he wants. But of course you don't. It's a challenge." It's no accident that flexible organizations emphasize "human relations skills" and offer "interpersonal" training. Strip away the psychological fluff and a solid need remains; in these environments people need to be proactive when faced with ill-defined circumstances.

Which might suggest that human relations of an open sort matter more in flexible organizations—a suggestion which the prophets of the fresh page have taken to be proven fact; in fluid structures, sensitivity replaces duty. A third comparison between the MP3 player and the flexible organization makes clear why mutual awareness becomes colored by anxiety and, all too often, institutionalized paranoia.

In an MP3 player, the laser in the central processing unit is boss. While there is random access to material, flexible performance is possible only because the central processing unit is in control of the whole. Similarly, in a flexible organization, power becomes concentrated at the center; the institution's central processing unit sets the tasks, judges results, expands and shrinks the firm. New analytic technologies have enabled firms to engage in what Michel Foucault has called "panoptic surveillance"; these technologies put real-time maps of resources and performance on screen. This computerized surveillance differs, however, from the control envisaged by Taylor and efficiency experts in an earlier era.

In order to deliver quick, flexible results, work groups have to be given a certain measure of autonomy. Indeed, the firm will try to motivate autonomy through internal markets; the center sets the terms of competition between teams in writing a piece of computer code, raising money, or designing a product, then five or six teams compete against each other to do it. In Taylor's way of thinking, based on pyramid form, this would be highly inefficient, since you have duplication of effort, but in the new, flexible way of thinking, what matters is producing the best result as quickly as possible. That's a more modern measure of efficiency. This kind of internal competition leads to what the economist Robert Frank calls "winner-takes-all" rewards: the big prizes come only to the winning team, and there are few or no consolation prizes.[12]

The system produces high levels of stress and anxiety among workers, as I and many other researchers have found. All competition, of course, breeds stress; the stakes are raised in winner-takes-all markets. Internal markets raise the anxiety stakes again higher, since the line between competitor and colleague becomes unclear. The temps I've interviewed who are better at managing stress can do so just because they don't emotionally belong to the firm. In contrast to the administrative assistant quoted above, one of my subjects at a West Coast high-tech firm complained that the winning team in an internal competition "took advantage" of her need to go home early to attend to her young children; they knew they could "win" because of her small family. They were false colleagues.

One way to contrast this situation to the pyramidal firms I studied thirty years ago lies in the emotional difference between anxiety and dread. Anxiety attaches to what might happen; dread attaches to what one knows will happen. Anxiety arises in ill-defined conditions, dread when pain or ill-fortune is well defined. Failure in the old pyramid was grounded in dread; failure in the new institution is shaped by anxiety. When firms are reengineered, employees frequently have no idea of what will happen to them, since modern forms of corporate restructuring are driven by issues of debt and stock-price value generated in financial markets, rather than by the internal workings of the firm. All too frequently the engineers of change have little idea of what to do once the merger or sale is effected. This indeterminacy spreads anxiety throughout the ranks, which the merchant bankers or investors are in no position to clarify. One near-certainty is that inequality within the firm will intensify. But inequality of a special sort.

•   •   •

Inequality has become the Achilles' heel of the modern economy. It appears in many forms: massive compensation of top executives, a widening gap between wages at the top and the bottom of corporations, the stagnation of the middle layers of income relative to those of the elite. Winner-takes-all competition generates extreme material inequality. These inequalities of wealth are matched within certain kinds of firms by a widening social inequality.

In bureaucracies in the throes of reorganization, the erasure of intermediate layers of bureaucracy can erase the communication chain by which power is interpreted as it passes downward, and information is modulated as it passes upward. Once reformed, the flexible firm can map out this more disconnected territory. The center governs the periphery in a specific way. On the periphery people are on their own in the process of laboring, without much interaction up and down the chain of command; there is nothing like a social relationship between a Thai shoe-stitcher and a Milanese fashionista; they transact, to refer to Soros, rather than relate. Those at the periphery are answerable to the center only for results. This distanced relation is, *in fine*, the geography of globalization. At the opposite extreme, in a bureaucratic pyramid, would stand the paternalistic employer. In terms of wealth and power, a paternalist like Henry Ford was indeed as unequal to workers on the assembly line as any modern global mogul. In sociological terms, however, he was closer to them, just as the general on the battlefield was connected to his troops. The sociological idea here is that inequality translates into distance; the greater the distance—the less a felt connection on both sides—the greater the social inequality between them.

Consulting work is an excellent case for understanding how social distance operates on the ground. Consultants are an essential ingredient in modern bureaucratic power, lubricating its machinery. In principle, consultants are meant to provide objective advice and strategy; in practice they do the painful work of re-organizing activities throughout the peripheries of the organization—forced retirements, abolition of departments, new duties for employees who survive.

Georgina Born of Cambridge University has done perhaps the best modern ethnography of consulting.[13] She studied the British Broadcasting Corporation in the 1990s, as a reform-minded executive, John Birt, brought in the McKinsey consulting group for a year to reshape the BBC ten-year strategy document. The consultants, mostly young men with recent MBA degrees, learned about the business in the process of reengineering it. Strategy meant formally altering the processes by which the BBC worked—who reported to whom, what they reported, what they had to report. The McKinsey consultants took little responsibility, however, for implementing these changes, nor did they deal with the human consequences of change; among these consequences were large numbers of people shifted from areas in which they had developed expertise to areas in which they were driving blind. In this "creative industry" the consultants themselves lacked much understanding of creative work, so tended to dismiss its inherent value. The consultants were paid, then departed, leaving the organization in turmoil, increasing social distances within the BBC. These human disconnections in the midst of change in turn dramatically increased employees' feelings of anxiety.

What have top managements to gain by employing consultants? In part, the consultant's presence sends an ideological signal that power is being exercised—a message of corporate will and determination. In the profit sector, sending such a signal is important: institutional disruption serves as a sign to investors that something is happening to the firm—change, no matter how ill-defined—which often raises the stock price. But the increase of social distance, within firms, has another benefit.

By hiring consultants, executives at the center of the MP3 machine can shift responsibility for painful decisions away from themselves. The central unit commands but avoids accountability. In practice, few consultants subsequently join the firms they reorganize, and thus they too avoid being held to account. This divorce between command and accountability explains the long political reach of consulting practices. In the wake of the breakdown of the Soviet empire in 1989, nations were subjected to something of the same treatment as the BBC. In Poland and Russia, teams of consultants descended on state ministries to dissolve or convert them into private businesses. The Harvard academic Jeffrey Sachs treated Poland as a free-market experiment, but he did not remain in Poland as a government official. Having reorganized the economy, which is still trying to recover from this experiment, Sachs returned to the United States and moved on to problems in the environment.

In creating social distances which divorce control from accountability, consulting reveals a fundamental shifting of bureaucratic ground, a reformatting of inequality, increasing social distance. Power can become concentrated at the top, but authority does not thereby increase.

Authority and Control

Authority names a complex social process of dependency.[14] A person possessed of authority differs from a tyrant, who deploys brute force to be obeyed. As Weber longer ago observed, someone possessed of authority elicits voluntary obedience; his or her subjects believe in him. They may believe him to be harsh, cruel, unjust, but still, something more is present. People below come to rely on those above them. In charismatic forms of authority, those below believe that the authority figure will complete and enable what is incomplete and disabled in themselves; in bureaucratic forms of authority, they believe that institutions will take responsibility for them.

Armies offer a clear case of both charismatic and bureaucratic authority. Soldiers die willingly for officers possessed of superior will or courage, and they will die also for mediocre officers; the office invests the incompetent with authority. This duality is familiar to any reader of Joseph Heller's war novel *Catch-22*, in which the cynical view of troops about their incompetent superiors coexists with voluntary obedience. Civil hierarchies produce the same duality of authority. In a classic study of the bureaucratic work pyramid, Reinhard Bendix found employees relying on bosses for advice, asking for directions, seeking approval, even though outside working hours they made catty remarks about their employers' personalities.

The MP3 institution may celebrate the charismatic leader yet does not invite institutional authority. In part this is due to the way executives behave, when they themselves act like consultants. Rapid turnover at the top can have this effect; there is then no one in power who has shown commitment to the organization, who has experience of its problems, who can serve as a witness of the labors of those below. In part, the sheer disconnect between center and periphery dispels the belief, at the periphery, that a particular human being or definable group at the center is really in charge. I found, in this regard, that employees at a financial services firm regarded "rule by e-mail" exceptionally obnoxious; all too frequently people received e-mails informing them they were being shifted, or even fired— "too chicken" as one person said, "to tell me to my face." Pushing away responsibility has a further dimension.

In going through the personnel records of a high-tech firm with a revolving-door management, I was struck by how often the words *needy* and *dependant* were used as negatives. One personnel manager told me she looked for something like self-discipline without dependency in her employees. This makes institutional sense. The operations are fragmented, either geographically on the periphery in big firms or internally in medium-sized organizations when many unconnected activities go on at the same time. Under such conditions people are indeed on their own, left to their own devices as how best to respond to targets, commands, and performance evaluations from the center. The celebration of self-management is, though, hardly innocent. The firm need no longer think critically about its own responsibilities to those whom it controls.

Just as the cutting-edge organizations are special cases, so are such employees. For some people the combination of increased central control and diminished authority works brilliantly. Cutting-edge organizations want to attract entrepreneurially minded young people; these are good places for people of all ages whose desire to serve as figures of authority is low. Those whom we have found most comfortable practically in these institutions are people with high technical skills. If they become disaffected, they can easily transport these skills somewhere else. Computer service-workers, floor traders in brokerage firms, editors and creative directors in advertising all fit this mold.

My colleague Michael Laskaway has found, among young entrepreneurs, that comfort in low-authority firms is short-lived. As middle age looms and children, mortgages, and school fees appear, the need for structure and predictability in work grows greater. Correspondingly, the employee now wants someone above who is responsive to the workers' own adult responsibilities.

The divorce between power and authority becomes more generally problematic when cutting-edge institutions become a model for public institutions. Reformers of the welfare state in Britain and Germany have taken the highly centralized, diminished authority model as a goal in providing benefits; correspondingly, the sick and the elderly can be stigmatized for showing neediness. But in the public realm, concentrated power with low authority becomes a danger to those in power. For legitimacy, they can rely only on their charisma; reformers who lack charisma are seen as arbitrary, institutions which eschew responsibility are seen, exactly, to be irresponsible.

Later in this chapter, I will try to unpack the crisis of legitimacy which occurs when the new capitalist model for enterprise is applied to the public realm. Here I want to remain within the social life of the new economic institution itself. The structural changes involved in taking apart the iron cage of bureaucracy produce three social deficits.

Three Social Deficits

The three deficits of structural change are low institutional loyalty, diminishment of informal trust among workers, and weakening of institutional knowledge. Each singly is all too tangible in the lives of ordinary workers. They relate to one another in terms of a somewhat abstract intellectual tool.

This tool sociology calls social capital—and as is the way of sociologists, we do not agree among ourselves about what it means. One school, represented by Robert Putnam, defines social capital in terms of people's voluntary engagements in social and civic organizations.[15] Another school, developed by Alejandro Portes and Harrison White, focuses on networks—in the family, education, and labor. While Putnam stresses the *willingness* to become involved, Portes and White weigh social capital in terms of how deeply and widely people *are* involved in networks, whether by will or necessity.[16] My own view of social capital, closer to Portes and White than to Putnam, emphasizes the *judgments* people make of their involvements. In my view, social capital is low when people decide their engagements are of poor quality, high when people believe their associations are of good quality.

Loyalty is a prime test of this version of social capital. Military organizations have high social capital, evinced when people are willing to sacrifice their lives out of loyalty to the institution or to the network of soldiers within an army. Cutting-edge institutions in civil society lie at the opposite extreme. They elicit extremely low levels of loyalty. The reason is not far to seek. If an employer tells you that you are on your own, that the institution will not help you out when you are in need, why should you feel much loyalty to it? Loyalty is a participatory relationship; no business plan alone, beautiful or logical as it may be, will earn the loyalty of those on whom it is imposed, simply because the employees have not participated in its gestation.

In the recent economic downturn, businesses learned the practical consequences of low loyalty. The boom had made it possible for companies to use the Internet to find suppliers or subcontractors for the best deal; when business was good it could be indeed conducted as in short-term transactions rather than long-term relationships. During the boom, business gurus had announced with a hint of pride that "loyalty is dead," and that each vigorous employee ought to behave like an entrepreneur.[17] When business became bad, however, companies needed suppliers and subcontractors to extend credit, to carry debt on the books —but why should someone else take on these problems? No network of mutual loyalty had developed.

Now as the business cycle moved downward, businesses needed employees to make sacrifices for the sake of the firm by taking pay or benefit cuts. The airline industry in America and Britain served as a prime example, joined by the media and technology sectors. But employees balked. British Airways, for instance, almost bankrupt, experienced frequent wildcat strikes by service workers who didn't care whether or not it went under. Even when other employees acted practically to save their own jobs, they made few positive efforts to help companies survive.

Loyalty is a necessary ingredient in surviving the business cycle; low social capital matters most practically to firms in the effort to fight off predators. For employees themselves, deficits of loyalty exacerbate stress, particularly, we found, the stress of working long hours. The stretched-out, intense workday can seem without purpose; pressure becomes depressing rather than stimulating. "Long hours don't do me any good," a designer in advertising told me, "and I don't give a shit about this firm, so what's the point?" Some recent large-scale studies in Britain of employees working more than ten hours a day elaborates the sentiment. Pressure becomes a self-contained, deadening experience in firms with low social capital, and employees who experience pressure on these terms are far more likely to become alcoholic, to divorce, or to exhibit poor health than people working more than ten hours daily in high-loyalty firms.

A second social deficit, less obvious than low loyalty, concerns trust. Trust comes in two shapes, formal and informal. Formal trust means one party entering into a contract, believing the other party will honor its terms. Informal trust is a matter of knowing on whom you can rely, especially when a group is under pressure: who will go to pieces, who will rise to the occasion. Informal trust takes time to develop. In a team or a network, small clues about behavior and character appear only incrementally; the mask we present to others normally conceals how reliable we will prove in a crisis. In bureaucracies oriented to the short term, time to develop this understanding of other people is often lacking. A team with a six-month life span reveals much less about how people are likely to behave under stress than a network whose life span can be measured in years.

I witnessed the strength and weakness of informal trust in two industrial accidents separated by thirty years. In the first, in an old-style factory, a fire burst out, and the circuit of fire nozzles turned out to be broken. Line workers knew each other well enough to decide who could do what. The managers squawked out orders, but in the emergency nobody paid attention to them; damage to the plant was soon brought under control by a strong informal network. Thirty years later I happened to be in a Silicon Valley plant when the air-conditioning system began sucking in rather than expelling noxious gases, an unforeseen design disaster in this high-tech building. The work teams did not hold together. Many people dangerously stampeded for the exits, while others, more courageous, were at a loss as to how to organize themselves. In the aftermath, the managers, many of whom had responded well, realized that this plant of thirty-two hundred people was, as one said, only "superficially organized on paper."

More ordinary forms of pressure at work can produce deficits of informal trust. Businesses which have to react quickly to changes in consumer demand often diminish informal trust, since the personnel of work teams has to change frequently. Corporate reengineering of an institution, whether business or a government agency, can also radically decrease informal trust, since reorganization of personal relations comes abruptly from above and from outside.

Low informal trust is an organizational deficit rather than a simple issue of personal character in that it revolves around organized time. Here a malign practice from the old world of work has passed into the new. When Taylor and other supposedly scientific work analysts did time-and-motion studies, they focused on miniaturized time, that is, how much could be done in the shortest amount of time. They seldom studied the months or years of an organization's life, perhaps because they took the durability of the firm for granted. Now that larger assumption cannot be made, and still micromanagement of time remains the focus. For employees in such volatile firms, not really knowing other workers can only increase anxiety; these volatile firms, for all their emphasis on the surface aspects of cooperation, are more impersonal and opaque than institutions in which people make long-term careers with others whom they come to know well. The result is networks which can easily tear apart.

The third social deficit concerns the weakening of institutional knowledge. One vice of the old bureaucratic pyramid was its rigidity, its offices fixed, its people knowing what exactly what was expected of them. The virtue of the pyramid was, however, accumulation of knowledge about how to make the system work, which meant knowing when to make exceptions to the rules or contriving back-channel arrangements. As in armies, so in big civilian bureaucracies, knowing how to manipulate the system can become an art form. Often the people who have the most institutional knowledge of this sort are low down the corporate hierarchy. In factories, shop-floor stewards possess it more than their white-shirted bosses; in offices, secretaries and personal assistants are bearers of institutional knowledge, in hospitals nurses are famously more competent at bureaucracy than the doctors they serve. This kind of institutional knowledge complements informal trust; in time, as experience accumulates, the bureaucrat learns how to oil bureaucratic wheels.

Yet in the reform of bureaucratic pyramids, these low-level functionaries are often the first to be let go. Management imagines that computerized technology can take their place, yet most business software applies rather than adapts rules. The consequence can be what the systems analyst Claudio Ciborra calls "drifting effects." He explains this by citing the application of an organizational program, Lotus Notes, to four different businesses. In the Zeta Corporation, which did not substitute the program for people, the results were positive, as employees had a new tool for knowledge sharing. In Unilever, where low-level staff were replaced by the program, the result was too much formalization; in Telecom, similarly reengineered, there appeared lack of knowledge sharing, and in EDF "interfunctional rivalry." In the positive case, Ciborra argues, institutional knowledge increased thanks to the computer application, while in the negative cases it decreased because its human bearers were eliminated.[18]

New information systems always promise greater efficiency in an organization—particularly appealing to consultants, who lack the kind of institutional knowledge which accumulates through experience. Yet this is a naive promise. The machines are not themselves the enemy; a program like Lotus Notes can in fact greatly increase knowledge of the organization, if control and adaptation are left to ordinary users. In most reengineering, however, the tendency is increasingly to limit access to reconfiguration, as control of the program is confined to the institution's upper echelons.

•   •   •

These three social deficits—of loyalty, informal trust, and adaptive information—are not news to many managers. The legal scholar Mark Roe argues that the root of the problem lies in "the separation of ownership from control"; it is to him a problem rooted in the very size of firms, whether old-style pyramid or new-style MP3. The manager is not allowed to assume effective, long-term responsibility for the firm; impatient investors hold the real reins of power.[19] The effective manager instead wants to build loyalty, trust, and institutional knowledge within the firm, all of which require time. Most dedicated managers, in my experience, attest to the conflict and in this form. What's missing from institutions of low social capital is equally often awareness of *who* builds social capital in a firm;

social capital is built from the bottom up. A firm's culture, like all culture, depends on how ordinary people make sense of an institution, not the explanation which those at the top decree. In the peculiar institutions at capitalism's cutting edge, decrees are issued and reissued quickly, constantly; the scope for interpretation, among ordinary workers, decreases, and the process of interpretation—of making sense of these chameleon organizations—becomes more and more arduous.

The most difficult problem of building a sense of social inclusion, for those not in control of institutions, lies in the issue of work identity.

Understanding Oneself

Emile Durkheim long ago, in *The Division of Labor*, understood the immense value individuals attach to being able to categorize themselves. As a general rule, identity concerns not so much what you do as where you belong. In the 1970s, it seemed clear to me that labor mattered deeply to working-class men I interviewed as a source of family and communal honor, quite apart from whatever satisfactions a job brought in itself. Their work identity, that is, lay in the social consequences of their labor. To working-class women in the labor market, it seemed to me then, the dignity afforded by work seemed to matter less. And to middle-class workers, the contents of a job appeared to matter more than to those below. In retrospect I see that I got both class and gender wrong. I got it wrong then, and time has since sorted things out differently today.

Many working-class women were indeed entering and leaving the labor force sporadically, to make ends meet at home, and for these women work was just an instrument. But others permanently labored, and to them work mattered in the same familial and communal ways it did to men. Claire Siegelbaum has pointed out one reason for my error: working-class women tended not to share the importance of their work with their spouses, since to do so would challenge sex roles in the family.

I also got wrong the investment of middle-class men in the substance of their work. A number of studies in the early 1980s showed there was little difference between manual laborers and nonprofessional white-collar workers in the desire for job satisfaction. Seniority and titles counted for people who worked with paper in much the same way as for people who worked with their hands.[20] I'd mistaken the world of the professional elite for that of the larger middle class.

What I had got right was the importance of the organizations themselves. The pyramids had relatively clear and stable identities, and this mattered to workers in their sense of themselves. Well-run companies provided a sense of pride, poorly run companies provided at least an orientation: you came to know about yourself in relation to the frustrations or anger you experienced in an *anchored* social reality outside yourself.

For black and immigrant workers, in both America and Britain, fixed-work bureaucracies had a further meaning: these institutions served as a promissory note for social inclusion. In America, a black laborer who gained seniority rights acquired a personally important weapon against the old formula, last-hired and first-fired. In both countries, working for the government in particular meant blacks and immigrants achieved the status of officialdom. A generation ago it was sometimes argued, more broadly, that outsiders have a weaker sense of work identity than those securely sheltered within the legal system or within the dominant culture; in America, it was often said of American male blacks that they lacked a work ethic. We now know this to be completely wrong: the research of William Julius Wilson and his colleagues has shown that access to secure work constituted then and constitutes now the single greatest life goal for disempowered black males.[21]

The advent of a new bureaucratic form has not statistically abolished inclusive jobs in large numbers, nor has work identity of the older sort eroded. As in an earlier generation, the value most people put on their labor lies in its familial or communal results. What living in the special circumstances of leading-edge work has disturbed in the larger culture could be called the moral prestige of work stability. The sociologist Kathleen Newman has noted this at the lowest levels of fluid work, the realm of so-called McJobs—flipping hamburgers or clerking in stores. Access to such paid work is a positive for unskilled young people, but they are troubled if they move only slowly upward; the labor seems a dead end even when it in fact opens a door.[22] That impatience reflects a shift in the larger culture's value system, one in which stability as such increasingly lacks moral prestige. Slightly higher up the occupational scale, work in government bureaucracy has become infected with the same stain, so that manual

service jobs are no longer attractive to many youngsters. This is a sector—in nursing, school maintenance,
and transport—increasingly left to immigrant workers,
who focus on stability and its rewards rather than on
the cultural characterization of the work itself.

In the middle class, the issue of moral prestige is
more transparent. Risk-taking is emphasized in the
formation of young people for careers in business; an
increasing percentage of young people respond to that
appeal at the expense of careers in teaching or other
civil service jobs. I don't mean to reduce the crisis in
public sector recruitment just to a matter of values; pay
and conditions of employment play a large role. What
culture does is diminish a young person's belief in the
character of such work, belief that one would achieve
respect in the larger society by virtue of working as a
bureaucrat.

Had risk become a dominant value, we should expect temps, serial workers, and others who float below
the cutting-edge elite in the same fluid work time to
enjoy enhanced status. As I discovered when research-
ing *Corrosion of Character*, temps do often find the first
few years of floating labor satisfying. But as a more per-
manent condition they find floating labor to be frus-

trating. They want someone to want them permanently; participating in a social structure comes to matter more than personal mobility. This mirrors the same problem felt in the passage from being a young, unattached entrepreneur to becoming a middle-aged entrepreneur with a mortgage. The moral prestige of cutting-edge labor is a talisman of success which is hard for people, below elite levels, to practice as a life project. In this, the conditions of time, enshrined in labor at the cutting edge, intersect with perhaps the most famous of all modern formulations of work identity as moral value, that of Weber's *Protestant Ethic*.

The time-engine driving the Protestant Ethic is delayed gratification in the present for the sake of long-term goals. This time-engine Weber believed to be the secret of the iron cage, people immuring themselves within fixed institutions because they hoped finally to empower themselves in a future reward. Delayed gratification makes possible self-discipline; you steel yourself to work, unhappily or not, because you are focused on that future reward. This highly personalized version of the prestige of work requires a certain kind of institution to be creditable; it has to be stable enough to deliver the future rewards, its managers have to remain in place as witnesses to your performance.

The new paradigm makes nonsense of delayed gratification as a principle of self-discipline; those institutional conditions are missing. The turn of the economic wheel in recent years has brought this out in stark relief. The downturn has clarified and sharpened a phenomenon more hidden during the boom: when things get bad, people at the top have more room for maneuver and adaptation than those below; in troubled companies, the managerial network is thicker and richer, allowing those above more easily to escape. The result is that the rewarding witnesses have, like Nietzsche's absconding God, fled the bureaucratic scene. In high-tech, finance, and the media this managerial revolving door has meant that the steady, self-disciplined worker has lost his audience.

The problem of delayed gratification is rendered more largely problematic, in North America and across Europe, because many private pension funds have collapsed, and government pensions schemes are imperiled. Saving for the future, the essence of the Protestant Ethic, is vitiated by the weakness of these structures, no longer safe havens.

The erosion of the Protestant Ethic is perhaps sharpest in the realm of personal strategic planning. My colleague Michael Laskaway has recently completed a study comparing the career planning of young adults in the 1970s to those today.[23] Both groups are university-educated and ambitious; the striking difference between them is how their ambitions are focused. The group from an earlier generation thought in terms of long-term strategic gains, the contemporary group in terms of their immediate prospects. More finely, the older group was able to verbalize goals, whereas the contemporary group had trouble finding language to match their impulses. In particular, the older group could define its eventual gratifications, while the contemporary group dealt in more amorphous desires.

Such a finding should not surprise us. In the 1970s, thinking in strategic narratives accorded with the way institutions were perceived; such thinking, for an ambitious young person, does not accord with the way leading-edge institutions appear today. The issue is the model: even when young people now enter relatively fixed work pyramids, their point of reference is the fluid model, present-oriented, evoking possibility rather than progression.

Here class counts for everything. A child of privilege can afford strategic confusion, a child of the masses cannot. Chance opportunities are likely to come to the child of privilege because of family background and educational networks; privilege diminishes the need to strategize. Strong, extensive human networks allow those at the top to dwell in the present; the networks constitute a safety net which diminishes the need for long-term strategic planning. The new elite thus has less need of the ethic of delayed gratification, as thick networks provide contacts and a sense of belonging, no matter what firm or organization one works for. The mass, however, has a thinner network of informal contact and support, and so remains more institution-dependent. It's sometimes said that the new technology can somewhat correct this inequality, electronic chat rooms and affinity groups supplying the information a young person would need to seize the moment. In the work world, at least at the moment, this is not the case. Face-to-face matters. This is why techies go to so many conventions, and, more consequently, why people working from home, connected to the office only by computer, so often are left out of informal decision gathering and decision making.

In general, the lower down in an organization, the thinner one's network, the more a person's survival requires formal strategic thinking, and formal strategic thinking requires a legible social map.

• • •

One way to sum up the issue, so far developed: the erosion of social capitalism has created a new formulation for inequality. The fresh-page thesis has argued change would set people free from the iron cage. The old institutional structure has indeed been taken apart in the special realm of flexible organizations. In its place comes a new geography of power, the center controlling the peripheries of power in institutions with ever fewer intermediate layers of bureaucracy. This new form of power eschews institutional authority, has low social capital. Deficits of loyalty, informal trust, and accumulated institutional knowledge result in cutting-edge organizations. For individuals, even while the value of working can remain strong, the moral prestige of work itself is transformed; labor at the cutting edge disorients two key elements of the work ethic, deferred gratification and long-term strategic thinking.

In these ways, the social has been diminished; capitalism remains. Inequality becomes increasingly tied to isolation. It is this peculiar transformation which has been seized upon by politicians as the model of "reform" in the public realm.

CHAPTER TWO

Talent and the Specter of Uselessness

A defining image of the Great Depression in the 1930s was photographs of men clustered outside the gates of shuttered factories, waiting for work despite the evidence before their eyes. Those photographs still disturb because the specter of uselessness has not ended; its context has changed. Large numbers of people in the rich economies of North America, Europe, and Japan want work but can't find it.

In the Great Depression individuals believed in a personal remedy for uselessness which transcended any government nostrum: their children should get an education and a special skill which would make the young always needed, always employed. Today, too, that is the armor people seek, but again the context has changed. In the "skills society" many of those who face unemployment are educated and skilled, but the work they want has migrated to places in the world where skilled labor is cheaper. So skills of quite another sort are needed.

In the following pages I want to explore how the specter of uselessness relates to the solution of education and formation, a person's *Bildung* as the Germans put it. The connection requires asking some basic questions: What does skill—more comprehensively, talent—mean? How does being a talented person translate into economic value? These questions bridge economics, psychology, and sociology; their scope is so large that I can't hope to find answers, only clarify problems.

The specter of uselessness first took its modern turn in the development of cities, whose migrants no longer had land to work under their feet. People moved to cities as dispossessed agricultural refugees, hoping that mechanized factories would provide for them. However, in London, to take a representative example, in 1840 there were six male laborers for every available unskilled factory job. David Ricardo and Thomas Malthus were the first modern theorists of uselessness, Ricardo probing how markets and industrial machines reduced the need for labor, Malthus reckoning the perverse consequences of population growth. Neither envisioned brains as a remedy for the oversupply of hands. In the early industrial era very few laborers could enter higher education; upward mobility was rare. And even the most enlightened reformers did not believe the bulk of the masses could otherwise, at work, become usefully skilled. Malthus, like Adam Smith before him and John Ruskin after him, viewed factory labor as brain-deadening. So as cities swelled, uselessness was viewed as a necessary, if tragic, consequence of growth.

One of the real achievements of modern society is to remove the opposition between *mass* and *mental*. Educational institutions have improved standards of numeracy and literacy on a scale which the Victorians could not have imagined. The Depression-era dream of a talented poor boy—or rarely, girl—becoming a doctor or lawyer is one which today seems, as it were, a routine sort of dream. Rough estimates put the upward mobility of children of unskilled laborers into the lower middle class at about 20 percent in Britain and America, about 15 percent in Germany, and about 30 percent in China—not a lot, countervailed by downward mobility, but much greater than in the first industrial era.

These indubitable achievements only pose Ricardo's early proposition in a new and painful form. The skills economy still leaves behind the majority; more finely, the education system turns out large numbers of unemployable educated young people, at least unemployable in the domains for which they have trained. In its modern form, Ricardo's proposition is that the skills society may need only a relatively small number of the educated who possess talent; especially in the cutting-edge realms of high finance, advanced technology, and sophisticated services. The economic machine may be able to run profitably and efficiently by drawing on an ever-smaller elite.

The Specter of Uselessness

Three forces shape the specter of uselessness as a modern threat: the global labor supply, automation, and the management of ageing. Each is not quite what it might at first glance seem.

When the press writes scare stories about the global labor supply draining jobs from rich to poor places, the story is usually presented as a "race to the bottom" simply in terms of wages. Capitalism supposedly looks for labor wherever labor is cheapest. This story is half wrong. A kind of cultural selection is also at work, so that jobs leave high-wage countries like the United States and Germany, but migrate to low-wage economies with skilled, sometimes overqualified, workers.

Indian call centers are a good example. The jobs in these centers are performed by people who are at least bilingual; they have refined their language skills so that the caller doesn't know whether she has reached Hartford or Bombay. Many call-center workers have had two or more years of university training; more, on the job they have been well trained. Indian call centers stress "stretch-learning," which is to have so much information in one's head that one can answer most conceivable questions quickly, thus enabling a rapid turnover in calls. The centers also train their workers in "human-resource skills," so that, for instance, impatience is never evident to a befuddled caller. The Indian workers are better educated and better trained than call-service workers in the West (excluding Ireland and

Germany, which operate at near Indian standard). The wages for this work are indeed abominable, paid to highly capable people.

Something of the same phenomenon appears in some industrial jobs which have migrated to the global South. Here a telling instance is automobile sub-assembly plants on the northern border of Mexico. The people doing very routine forms of labor are quite often highly skilled mechanics who have left auto-body shops to work on the assembly line. Up North, line laborers in the Mexican maquiladoras might be subforemen or foremen.

The most fearful image of the economic race to the bottom is of children leaving home and school to work in the sweatshops of the global South. This image is not false but, rather, incomplete. The labor market also looks for talent on the cheap. The appeal to employers of overqualified workers is the same in the global South as it is in the more developed world. Such capable workers prove good at problem solving, especially when something goes wrong with job routines.

In turn, the people who take these jobs are often quite entrepreneurial. In the Mexican maquiladoras, workers on the assembly line can establish a credit record after a few years of fixed-wage work, which can enable them then to go to banks for loans to start a small business of their own. The credit incentive is not quite as powerful in India, where the driving force is entrepreneurial subcontracting. In the Indian calls centers, many workers, once trained, have started small businesses which subcontract call-center work from the large foreign firms.

Of course it's important to keep this in perspective. Just as the bulk of global South jobs employ dispossessed farm laborers, so the hope of becoming a small businessman or businesswoman will remain for many just a hope—though the number of small-business start-ups in India, Mexico, China, and Indonesia has indeed increased almost exponentially in the past decade. What needs to be stressed is that these are not Ricardo's people. They cannot be classified simply as victims because they participate in the system and have an interest in it.

The reason I stress this is the consequence at home. They are of higher status than their peers in the global North, if less well paid. Their combination of motivation and training, their *Bildung*, constitutes a particular draw for employers. At home, the people who lose out would have to increase their human capital to compete, but few can do so; uncompetitive with these foreign peers, they face being no longer needed. The specter of uselessness here intersects with the fear of foreigners, which, beneath its crust of simple ethnic or race prejudice, is inflected with the anxiety that foreigners may be better armed for the tasks of survival. That anxiety has a certain basis in reality. *Globalization* names, among other things, a perception that the sources of human energy are shifting, and that those in the already developed world may be left out as a result.

The second specter of uselessness lurks in automation. The fear that machines will replace humans is ancient. The appearance of the first steam-driven spinning looms caused riots among French and British weavers; by the end of the nineteenth century it became painfully evident to many steelworkers that they would be "deskilled," machines doing their complicated labors, the men reduced to low-wage, routine tasks. In the past, however, the threat of automation was overdramatized.

The problem lay in the design and development of the machines themselves. Let me give a personal example. My grandfather, an industrial designer, worked for sixteen years (from 1925 to 1941) on the prototype of a robotic arm capable of one-millimeter manipulation: the gears and pulleys required for this high-tech machine cost a fortune, and the robotic arm itself needed constant readjustment. After wasting a fortune on my grandfather, his employer decided that skilled human fingers were cheaper. This story was repeated throughout the field of industrial design. The only real savings brought through true automation—in which most or all of the production process occurs via machines—appeared in those large-volume, heavy industries which produced goods like electric cables and metal pipes.

Thanks to the revolution in computing and in microelectronics, my grandfather's robotic arm is a tool which can now be quickly and effectively designed on screen; microprocessors take the place of the intricate, vulnerable gears and levers he contrived. In service labor, automation has converted the science fiction of the past into technological reality. I'm thinking of intelligent voice-answering devices—automation's future threat to the call center—or bar-code readers, which have transformed back-office accounting, inventory management, and front-of-counter sales. Electronics enable, further, the automation of quality control—the human eye replaced by the more rigorous laser censor.

Manufacturers use these technologies in a particular way. Automation permits manufacturers not only to respond quickly to changes in demand, since the machines can be quickly reconfigured, but also to execute quick turnarounds when demand changes and so keep inventories low.

Automation now truly delivers productivity gains and brings labor savings. Here are two examples: from 1998 to 2002, the Sprint Corporation increased its productivity 15 percent by using advanced voice-recognition software and increased its revenues year on year 4.3 percent, while cutting its payroll over this four-year period by 11,500 workers. In heavy industry, from 1982 to 2002 steel production in the United States rose from 75 million tons to 102 million tons even as the number of steelworkers dropped from 289,000 to 74,000. These jobs were not exported; for the most part, sophisticated machines took over.[1]

Which is to say, modern workers are finally facing the specter of automated uselessness.

In the past, when sociologists thought about automation, they imagined that new or more white-collar and human-service jobs would be created when pairs of hands were replaced by machines. This belief informed the "postindustrial" thesis advanced by both Daniel Bell and Alain Touraine.[2] The shift idea made sense, given the state of machines fifty years ago; for practical purposes, these machines were serviceable for only mechanical tasks. The machines we now possess can subtract labor across the board: the job losses at Sprint were in its human-service sector.

What sort of machines are these? When the watchmaker Jacques de Vaucanson fabricated a mechanical flute player in the mid–eighteenth century, the wonder of the robot seemed its *likeness* to a living human being. In the spirit of Vaucanson, much automation technology today still focuses on imitating the human voice or the human head—the latter in smart surveillance cameras which swivel and focus on anything the machine "sees" as unusual. But other technologies do not mimic human beings, notably computing technologies, which reckon at speeds no person could. The image of replacing a pair of hands by a machine is therefore inexact: as the work analyst Jeremy Rifkin has observed, the realm of uselessness expands as machines do things of economic value of which human beings are incapable.

Both global job migration and true automation are special cases which affect some, but not all, labor. Ageing defines a much more sweeping domain of uselessness. Everyone grows old, and, enfeebled, we all become at some point useless in the sense of unproductive. Age as a measure of uselessness is, however, finetuned in the modern economy in two ways.

The first is through sheer prejudice. When in the early 1990s I interviewed people in the advertising world my subjects worried that they would be "over the hill" by the time they turned thirty, "out of it" by the time they turned forty. The cutting-edge organization indeed tends to treat older employees as set in their ways, slow, losing energy. In advertising and media, the prejudice against age combines with views of gender: middle-aged women are particularly stigmatized as lacking drive; this combined prejudice appears also in financial services.

Ageism embodies an obvious paradox. Modern medicine enables us to live and to work longer than in the past. It made sense, in 1950, to set retirement at age fifty-five or sixty because the average male worker was likely to live only to his early seventies. Today, 50 percent of American males live into their early eighties, and most are healthy into their early seventies. When retirement age is kept to the old standard, males now spend fifteen to twenty years in which they could be productively employed but aren't. *Burnout* more accurately applies to the character of work than to the physical state of the worker. It would be perfectly possible, physiologically, for a middle-aged man to work as a global currency trader twelve hours a day—so long as he had no family or outside interests.

Age more directly touches the question of talent if we think about how long a skill lasts. If you are an engineer, how long will the skills you learned in university serve you? Less and less. "Skills extinction" has sped up not only in technical work, but in medicine, law, and various crafts. One estimate for computer repairmen is that they have to relearn their skills three times in the course of their working lifetimes; the figure is about the same for doctors. That is, when you acquire a skill, you don't have a durable possession.

Here labor-market economics intrudes in a particularly destructive way. An employer could choose either to retrain a fifty-year-old to get up to date or to hire a bright young thing of twenty-five already up to speed. It's much cheaper to hire the bright young thing— cheaper both because the older employee will have a higher salary base and because retraining programs for working employees are themselves expensive operations.

There's a further social wrinkle in this replacement process. Older employees tend to be more self-possessed and judgmental of their employers than younger workers. In retraining programs, older workers behave like other mature students, judging the value of the skill on offer and the ways it is taught in light of how they themselves have lived. The experienced worker complicates the meaning of what he or she learns, judging its worth in terms of his or her past. The Young Turk, by contrast, is a stereotype falsified by many studies of young workers themselves: lacking experience or standing in a firm, they tend to behave prudently, and if they don't like the conditions at a workplace, they tend to leave rather than resist, an option open to them since the young carry less family and community baggage. In firms, age thus makes an important difference between what the economist Albert Hirschmann has called "exit" and "voice." Young workers, more pliant, favor exit when discontented; older workers, more judgmental, give voice to their discontents.

Though Hirschmann sees this as a divide in all firms, it matters above all to those at the cutting edge, impatient as these businesses are with corporate second thoughts and measured introspection. Just because flexible firms expect employees to move around, and just because these firms do not reward service and longevity, the employer's choice is clear. The younger person is both cheaper and less trouble. The many firms which do invest in the skills of their employees over the long term tend to more traditional kinds of organization. Hirschmann's view is that such investments will be made particularly by firms which count loyalty as a corporate asset.

In those firms which do abandon the structures of social capitalism, the personal consequence of focusing on young talent is that as experience increases it has less value. I found in my interviewing that this slighting of experience was notably strong among consultants, who have a professional interest in thinking so. Their work in changing institutions requires suspicion of long-entrenched employees, whose accumulated institutional knowledge appears a barrier to swift change. Of course consultants do not come all in one piece; much of the work currently done by the Boston Consulting Group, for instance, accepts the inseparable connection between skill and experience. The effect of the boom in the 1990s, however, was to legitimate more superficial, quick-strike forms of consulting, embodied by the intervention in the BBC described by Georgina Born. In that strike, "skill" became defined as the ability to do something new, rather than to draw on what one had already learned to do. The consultant engineering sudden change has to draw on a key element in the new economy's idealized self: the capacity to surrender, to give up possession of an established reality.

The formula that, as experience increases it loses value, has a deeper reality in today's more chastened economy. Skills extinction is a durable feature of technological advance. Automation is indifferent to experience. Market forces continue to make it cheaper to buy skills fresh rather than to pay for retraining. And the draw of capable workers in the global South cannot be stemmed by the worker in the global North through the invocation of his or her experience.

These conditions combined give the specter of

uselessness solid substance in the lives of many people today. The brute mantra of "skill" cannot, alone, address them. Before addressing what specific kind of skill could address them, I need to relate this economic overview to the public sphere.

• • •

The specter of uselessness poses a challenge to the welfare state—the state broadly conceived as providing benefits to those in need. What will it offer people who are cast aside?

The record of response in the late twentieth century was not good. Even in countries like Britain and Germany, which have good-quality job retraining programs, it proved difficult to cure unemployment resulting from automation. The twentieth-century welfare state treated automation ineptly because policymakers suffered a failure of imagination. The planners failed to understand how fundamentally automation could change the very nature of the productive process. In the steel industry, for instance, the same forces which contracted the foundry reduced the office staff. Not only did government shy away from the enormity of this transformation; labor unions resisted thinking the matter through, focusing on job protection for existing workers rather than on shaping the future workforce. The American labor negotiator Theodore Kheel, founder of Automation House, spoke as a prophet in the wilderness when he argued to Western governments that the only "remedy" for true automation was to make paid jobs out of previously unpaid work like child care and community service.

The welfare state proved equally inept at dealing with age. The development of publicly funded pension and medical systems in the twentieth century can be understood as a form of wealth redistribution, shifting benefits from younger to older generations. Now the increasing longevity of old people strains this wealth redistribution, as does the falling birthrate in developed societies, so that fewer workers pay into the system. In terms of health care, the elderly today consume the lion's share of medical resources. Though just, financially the system has become, as everyone knows, unsustainable. In this quagmire, the age-ethos of the new capitalism is coming to play a primary role. This ethos diminishes the legitimacy of those in need. Recent surveys of young workers find they resent paying for their elders, and even someone as old as I am understands the resentment. The young have not been invited to vote on wealth redistribution.

Cultural attitudes have, ultimately, derailed the public realm from addressing the specter of uselessness. The "new man" takes pride in eschewing dependency, and reformers of the welfare state have taken that attitude as a model—everyone his or her own medical advisor and pension fund manager. Practically, as in private business, this cuts down on public responsibility. But it avoids an equally hard truth. Uselessness begets dependency; insufficiency breeds the need for help.

The most afflicted subjects researchers like Kathleen Newman and I have interviewed are middle-class, middle-aged men who, cut out of the old corporate culture, are having trouble finding a place in the new. It's important not to sentimentalize their condition in order to understand their problems. Few of those Newman and I have interviewed are self-pitying. When they set up as individual consultants, as many do, they vigorously pursue whatever leads come their way; their own "fear of falling," as Newman puts it, most are determined to address. But in their communities these marginal men become invisible. Others come to avoid asking them too many questions, for fear of raising the issue of uselessness. "Your friends talk sports and kids with you but avoid business," as one middle-aged computer programmer said to me. When marginalized men try to use the network of contacts they developed in their old firms, "it's like nobody knew you," another observed. The silence which surrounds their marginality marks America's greatest social taboo, failure, our unmentionable subject.

Most of the people we've interviewed know they need help, but don't know in what form it could come. Public institutions are indeed ill-adapted to deal with the downwardly mobile. The welfare state provides for those absolutely unemployed, but these men tend to be underemployed and so aren't taken into account. Marginality in the form of underemployment or semi-employment raises questions about human resources which escape statistical calculation, though the phenomenon is real enough: one estimate for the United States is that about a fifth of men in their fifties suffer underemployment. No figures exist for women in this age cohort, but given the prejudices about women workers in general, and middle-aged women workers in particular, underemployment for them surely cannot be less.

The issue of underemployment speaks to a more general problem in the public sphere. Discussions of welfare policy tend to use a rhetoric of abjection, of lost lives and the like; the simplest way to reform is to make a stark contrast between dependence and independence. But uselessness and marginality come in many shades of gray. By eliminating these colors, the state avoids the knotty issues of how to support the relatively needy, the somewhat dependent. Policies which addressed these knotty issues would have to be much more sophisticated and fined-tuned than they are at present. To put the matter abstractly, a welfare state can simplify itself by treating dependency, marginality, and need as absolutes.

At the end of this book, I want to address ways in which the public sphere could embrace the ambiguities of uselessness. To lay the ground for this, I need to elaborate more clearly two key terms which define people's talents: craftsmanship and meritocracy.

Craftsmanship and Meritocracy

Craftsmanship is a term most often applied to manual laborers and denotes the pursuit of quality in making a violin, watch, or pot. This is too narrow a view. Mental craftsmanship also exists, as in the effort to write clearly; social craftsmanship might lie in forging a viable marriage. An embracing definition of craftsmanship would be: doing something well for its own sake. Self-discipline and self-criticism adhere in all domains of craftsmanship; standards matter, and the pursuit of quality ideally becomes an end in itself.

Craftsmanship emphasizes objectification. When Nicolò Amati made a violin, he did not express himself through the violin. He made a violin. Whatever his feelings, he invested himself in that object, judging himself by whether or not the thing was made right. We are not interested in whether Amati was depressed or happy when he worked; we care about the cut of his f-holes and the beauty of his varnish. This is what objectification means: a thing made to matter in itself.

This objectifying spirit can give even low-level, seemingly unskilled laborers pride in their work. For instance, my student Bonnie Dill in the 1970s did a study of cleaning workers in Harlem—poorly paid black women often abused by their white employers downtown. At the end of the day, these women salvaged some fragment of self-worth in having cleaned a house well, though they were seldom thanked for it.[3] The house was clean. When I studied bakers in Boston in those same years, in a family-run bakery where the most junior members were treated roughly and pressed too hard by fathers and uncles, the results in the early morning similarly salved some of the upset: the bread was good.[4] While it's important not to romanticize the balm of craftsmanship, it matters equally to understand the consequence of doing something well for its own sake. Ability counts for something, by a measure which is both concrete and impersonal: clean is clean.

Understood this way, craftsmanship sits uneasily in the institutions of flexible capitalism. The problem lies in the last part of our definition, doing something for its own sake. The more one understands how to do something well, the more one cares about it. Institutions based on short-term transactions and constantly shifting tasks, however, do not breed that depth. Indeed the organization can fear it; the management code word here is *ingrown*. Someone who digs deep into an activity just to get it right can seem to others ingrown in the sense of fixated on that one thing—and obsession is indeed necessary for the craftsman. He or she stands at the opposite pole from the consultant, who swoops in and out but never nests. Moreover, deepening one's skills in any pursuit takes time. It usually takes three or four years for a young professional fresh out of university to sort out what was really serviceable in the subjects he or she studied. Deepening ability through practice sits at cross-purposes with institutions that want people to do many different things in short order. While the flexible organization thrives on smart people, it has trouble if they become committed to craftsmanship.

A good example of this conflict came to me in returning to a group of programmers I had once interviewed in a large but legally unmentionable software firm. These programmers resented the firm's practice of shipping out incompletely formulated software in versions then "corrected" through consumer struggles and complaints. While deeply antipathetic to unions, the programmers were developing a loose professional movement called craft in code, demanding that the company desist from this highly profitable but poor-quality practice. They wanted the time to get the programs right; their sense of meaningful work depended on doing this job well for its own sake.

Meritocracy poses a different kind of problem for the flexible organization. To understand the word we have to go far back in time.

When inheritance was the dominant fact of life for Europeans, there could be no concept of meritocracy in the easy sense we understand, that of giving to and rewarding a person for the job he or she does well. People inherited offices in the Church or the military just as they inherited land. Which is to say that positions were possessions. Which meant that it was a happy accident if a bishop happened to be religious but not a necessary qualification for the job. More gravely, in a world of armies and navies in which the officers inherited their ranks, an incompetent commander, no matter how much suffering he caused, could not be dismissed from his post; he owned it.

Inheritance did not smother the value placed on ability; rather, one's station in life and one's competence were parallel social worlds. It was the Renaissance artist who first began to build a bridge across the two. Michelangelo demanded his patrons submit to his genius—genius alone earning him rank. Benvenuto Cellini's *Autobiography* shows how the demand began to challenge institutions. As a youth, Cellini entered the guild of goldsmiths, an elite craft in which many other Renaissance painters began their careers. Entry into this guild was largely but not exclusively by inheritance; within the guild, people advanced only when someone higher up died or retired. Cellini (1500–71) jumped up, skipping the traditional progression, a man consumed by ambition for himself and his art. He accused guilds and other institutions which did not reward talent alone of being corrupt.

In that accusation sounds a new, modern note: the equation of talent with personal worth. Ability entails a kind of moral prestige. This note is social as well as personal. Craftsmanship fit easily within the medieval guild frame in that the apprentice as much as the master could seek to make something well for its own sake. Now talent measured a new sort of social inequality: *creative* or *intelligent* meant *superior* to others, a more worthy sort of person. Here lay the passage from craftsmanship to meritocracy.

Modern meritocracy took shape when institutions began to structure themselves on this sort of inequality. One way to date this birth lies in the career of Samuel Pepys, a middle-class Britain who in the 1660s was one of the first officials able to make his way up in government by virtue of the fact that he was smart; in particular, Pepys was good at adding and subtracting. In the Admiralty, he worked at provisioning the fleet; he had to reckon how many cannon balls and how much salt beef to put in ships. His claim was that he deserved this post because of his mathematical abilities, in preference to the Earl of Shrewsbury, whose second aunt was the niece of the then-reigning monarch. In the person of Pepys, as it were, Cellini had entered the portals of bureaucracy.

Military organization was the domain in which the notion of careers open to talent first made real headway. Like the bureaucratic pyramid, the military pointed the way for later careers open to talent in business. Military academies like St. Cyr, founded in the late seventeenth century, forced young officers to learn the mathematics which enable ballistic strategy. Military academies innovated in creating the first ability tests, a radical innovation in the eighteenth century. In both St. Cyr and the Prussian military academies, these tests were incorruptible, in the sense that the people tested appeared as numbers rather than names; an impersonal judgment was rendered on the contents of a person's brain. The tests thus provided a relatively objective measure of how capable an individual would be, certainly a more objective measure than family background or connections.

The military institutions thus not only discovered talent, they *objectified failure;* those who were stupid were eliminated no matter what their family background. This negative was in a way even more important than the positive. A bureaucratic procedure now measured something deep inside the individual, punishing him (and later her) for lack of ability. Absolute measures of incompetence only strengthened the "merit" of those who succeeded; an impersonal judgment determined personal worth.

Of course, class and cash still counted; up to the early nineteenth century throughout Europe a wealthy individual could buy an officer's commission—but now the professional soldier had come into being, with the professional's special prestige. The same structures came in time to govern the development of other professions in civil society, and with the same judgmental focus—law, medicine, accounting, education all eventually following the military model. Business came last: the modern business school completes the transformation begun in St. Cyr. Today businesses obsessively test and measure employees in the workplace, in order that talent be rewarded and, more consequently, failure certified and so legitimated.

Most arguments about preferential treatment in education and employment for categories of people, based on their race or class, turn on the way meritocracy took form as an impersonal judgment on individuals. On the one side the argument is that the dominant society discriminates against subordinate groups; on the other, that society possesses the technical instruments to determine who as a single individual has ability. Suffusing the debate is a highly personal judgment; the search for talent is no technical exercise. Merit is a far more personally intrusive category than competence.

The specific meaning of *merit* appears in a sweeping enquiry conducted over several decades of the mid-twentieth century by the American sociologist Otis Dudley Duncan. He asked first Americans and then people in other countries to rank the prestige of various occupations and found some striking uniformities: professionals like doctors, nurses, teachers, and social workers were more admired than business executives and stockbrokers, who made many times the salaries of these professionals; the teacher and nurse are also much more admired than politicians, who come in low on the list. The survey also found that skilled manual craftsmen like electricians and carpenters enjoy high prestige.

The reason for these ranks is straightforward. All the high-prestige workers have an ability developed within themselves, a skill whether mental or manual not dependent on circumstances. I suspect that if Duncan had substituted "statesman" for "politician," the political class would have risen in public estimation, because then the image is about a project which transcends manipulating circumstances and the public itself. Duncan's research illustrates the equation of occupational prestige with self-direction and autonomy more than with money or power. Merit in the work world is judged on this basis.

Cellini would, I think, have understood the formula merit equals autonomy. He would have understood that meritocracy transforms the spirit of craftsmanship into an invidious, highly personal comparison. But he would be baffled by the bureaucratic machinery which objectifies merit, the bureaucratization of talent, which has occurred in the development of modern society. This bureaucratic machinery of meritocracy has created an iron cage for ability, but it is a cell of solitary confinement.

• • •

To understand this machinery, we need ever to keep in mind what seems a self-evident fact, and a subtlety. The self-evident fact is that judgments of ability are Janus-faced: at one and the same time they single out ability and eliminate incompetence or lack of ability. This self-evident fact looks a little more problematic, though, if we recur to social capitalism as Bismarck first conceived it. His institutions promoted by merit—but also by seniority. The machinery aimed to include the masses, whether competent or not, so long as the masses put in their time and served the institution.

The search for talent in modern society, particularly in dynamic institutions, does operate within a framework of social inclusion. Just those tests, judgments, and milestones which reward the best serve as the basis for shedding others below this elite level. The Janus-faced search for talent is conspicuous when businesses are combined or when a single business decides to downsize. Bureaucracies often try to legitimate getting rid of layers or categories of people by claiming that only the worthy remain. Of course this can be a self-serving fiction, but such institutions are driven to justify impersonal, hasty, or arbitrary change on the

basis of shedding deadwood or other highly personalized judgments of who should remain.

The sociologist Pierre Bourdieu called this Janus-
faced relationship "distinction," the mass disabled or
penalized *tacitly* as educational, work, and cultural institutions confer elite status *explicitly*.[5] For Bourdieu
the real point of distinction is to create a mass in
shadow, by putting a spotlight on the elite. My own
view is that the spotlight shows a confused scene. This
is the subtle aspect of the meritocratic talent search—
the illumination and definition of talent itself.

In craftsmanship we are able to judge how well
someone performs by looking at the concrete results of
their labors. To displaced or discarded workers, those
results at least make legible why they have been cast
aside; the quality of Indian software programs and
Chinese manufactured goods are solid facts. It might
seem that the meritocracy machinery of testing and
on-the-job evaluation is equally solid. The measures,
after all, are standardized, numbers often taking the
place of names on tests to assure objectivity. But in
fact the bureaucratic machinery chases after something quite intangible; one can quantify what kinds of
work seem autonomous, for example, but not what spe-

cifically an autonomous act is. Craftsmanship requires mastering and owning a particular domain of knowledge; this new version of talent is not content-specific or content-determined. Cutting-edge firms and flexible organizations need people who can learn new skills rather than cling to old competencies. The dynamic organization emphasizes the ability to process and interpret changing bodies of information and practice.

Within the meritocratic scheme there is thus a soft center in evaluating talent; that soft center concerns talent conceived in a particular form, as potential ability. In work terms, a person's human "potential" consists in how capable he or she is in moving from problem to problem, subject to subject. The ability to move around in this way resembles the work of consultants, writ large. But potential ability cuts a larger cultural swath; it is a damaging measure of talent.

Potential Ability

The word *potential* is a red flag for anyone cursed by contact with the psychological clique that goes by the name "the human potential movement." Though too

often just a version of the self-help and self-improve-
ment business, exhorting its followers to discover the
real hidden inner you, the study of human potential
began as something quite serious. In the writings of
Abraham Maslow, for instance, human development
was viewed as a lifelong negotiation between the genetic capacities of an individual and his or her experience in society; in place of Freud's ideas about drives
and instincts, Maslow sought a more plastic understanding of the self's form in time.[6] His conviction
about continuous development appears today in the
writings of Amartya Sen and Martha Nussbaum on
human capabilities.[7] Like Maslow, the geneticist Richard Lewontin thinks of biology as furnishing a repertoire of human capacities used, or not used, variously
over the course of a lifetime as circumstances demand.[8]

The search for potential abilities can fall within
this project. Owing to prejudices of race, class, and gender, society may not tap into the talents of all its members: it should make that effort. This is a deeper claim
than serving the needs of a particular kind of institution—the flexible regime. Rather, it equates the discovery of potential ability with justice.

In the United States, this meritocratic claim lay behind the erection of a certain kind of testing, the Scholastic Aptitude Tests (SATs). A cliché about American education says that the country's schools put little emphasis on knowing something but a great deal of emphasis on knowing how to know. But the SAT set out, at first, not to eviscerate learning but to complete the project of "careers open to talent." In the years after the Second World War, the testers tried to figure out how to discover the potential to learn among young people from culturally deprived backgrounds. The testers' target was narrow, to recruit a new elite of raw talent for universities like Harvard.[9] The SAT drew on an old American ideal, Thomas Jefferson's belief in a "natural aristocracy," and certainly to Jefferson the search for talent was not meant to be Janus-faced: he believed a natural aristocracy could fit comfortably into the practices of democracy.[10] The SAT tests themselves began to transform this old ideal by framing ability in a new way.

By comparing the SAT to the tests given in the military academy of St. Cyr in the mid–eighteenth century, we understand what became new. St. Cyr asked the student, for instance, to perform a calculation using a quadratic equation and then asked the student to ex-

plain, in words, what went into the process of calculation. In the sections on "Patrie" (country), St. Cyr
asked for definitions of loyalty, courage, and sacrifice.
The testers graded the response as to whether the pupil
had given the true response. In other words, these were
tests of what we would call achievement, requiring for
the quadratic equations a preexisting mastery of how
to translate numbers into words (try it), for "Patrie,"
sufficient cultural impregnation to know just what
would count in the examiners' minds as true. There
were few surprises in these tests, students being informed well in advance exactly what knowledge they
would have to produce.

The SAT assumed a more innocent subject. Aptitude could be isolated from achievement by confront-
ing the subject with a problem to be solved, the test trying to minimize preexisting mathematical training;
the process of mathematical reasoning was to be under
the microscope. In the realm of words, the tests again
probe the process of thinking in words rather than
thinking correct thoughts. The mental world here is
operational, process divorced from content.

How this works is illustrative in a prep-book for
the SAT addressing the seemingly most objective part

of the test, the meaning of words. Here are two definitions offered for the word *incisive*:

> Following Huntley's *incisive* analysis, the bond traders
> were immediately galvanized into a frenzy of selling.

> Cheryl's *incisive* coverage of City Hall affairs made her a
> formidable candidate for a Pulitzer Prize.[11]

What is a bond trader or a Pulitzer Prize is treated as ir-
relevant cultural context. But the definitions paired together make for a puzzle. The first asks the teenager to
assume that bond traders are people who act on incisive
information, the second that incisive information earns
official rewards. Are bond traders therefore like liter-
ary prize judges? If not, is the point of incisive information that it was previously unknown—in that case,
the synonym for *incisive* should be *exposed,* not, as the
test coaches then recommend, *acute.*

The only practical way to deal with the ambiguities is not to dwell on them too much. The correct, objective answer lies on the adolescent's mental surface.
By probing meaning, digging deep, one risks losing
time and so doing a poor job on the exam; that's how
someone treating the test in a craftsmanlike spirit
would likely fare. The exam is "soft" in that sense at its

very heart—this purely operational thinking requires mental superficiality.

Yet exams like this are meant to test *innate* ability. The brilliant young girl lost in a Chicago ghetto is taken to have a capacity fresh and ready to respond; in the testing room, her inner capacity is meant to step forward, casting off the chains of circumstance. The idea of ability innocent of experience is, however, a fiction. Psychologists like Howard Gardner have further questioned why these two kinds of mental activities—mathematical and verbal activity—are treated as more innate than visual or auditory understanding: architects think in images, musicians in sounds. Even more elusive is emotional intelligence—hearing the intention beneath another's words, tact, empathy—a capacity which profoundly affects practical performance in the world. Most of all, to understand what all words mean, we, testers as well as subjects, assume they have referents.

The point of these objections is not to deny that ability exists or that there are differences between people. Rather, in the search to consummate the project of finding a natural aristocracy, the mental life of human beings has assumed a surface and narrowed form. Social reference, sensate reasoning, and emotional understanding have been excluded from that search, just as have belief and truth. By a perverse irony, the more modern testers have sought to eliminate cultural bias from their work, the thinner has become the innate ability they test.

It could be said in defense—and testers of ability do say so—that processes of verbal interpretation and mathematical reasoning are the practical skills a bright young woman from the urban ghetto needs to make her way in the world. That defense, and indeed the word *potential* in the phrase "potential ability," has a particular relation to the practices of flexible institutions.

These institutions, we have seen, privilege the kind of mental life embodied by consultants, moving from scene to scene, problem to problem, team to team. Team members themselves have to become adept at process work, since they will in time be moving around in the organization. There is a real talent required for such labor. It is the ability to think prospectively about what might be done by breaking context and reference—at its best, a work of imagination. At its worst, though, this talent search cuts reference to experience and the chains of circumstance, eschews sensate impressions, divides analyzing from believing, ignores the glue of emotional attachment, penalizes digging deep—a state of living in pure process which the philosopher Zygmunt Bauman calls "liquid modernity."[12] Which is just the social condition of work at the cutting edge.

Knowledge and Power

The formulation of potential ability leads back to the relation between talent and the specter of uselessness, a relationship which looks different once we have described the kind of knowledge which is now useful, particularly at the cutting edge of the economy.

The French philosopher Michel Foucault was the modern era's great analyst of the ways knowledge enables certain forms of power. He had in view the development of increasingly elaborated, dense knowledge which would serve the purpose of ever more complete control over individuals and groups; for instance, the development of psychiatry was in his view intimately linked to the spread of institutions of incarceration.[13] The Foucaultian scheme does not envisage superficial knowledge as a tool of power, and in this way does not quite describe the way potential ability is sought and practiced in modern meritocracy. But he illuminated an all-important fact about meritocracy: it disempowers the larger majority of those who fall under its rule.

When Michel Young coined the term *meritocracy* he meant to dramatize, painting crudely, a society in which a small number of skilled people can control an entire society. Foucault made a more detailed picture of this domination; the elite would get under the skin of the masses by making them feel that they did not understand themselves, that they were inadequate interpreters of their own experience of life. Tests of potential ability show just how deeply under the skin a knowledge system can cut. Judgments about potential ability are much more personal in character than judgments of achievement. An achievement compounds social and economic circumstances, fortune and chance, with self. Potential ability focuses only on the self. The statement "you lack potential" is much more devastating than "you messed up." It makes a more fundamental claim about who you are. It conveys uselessness in a more profound sense.

Just because the statement is devastating, organizations engaged in continual internal talent searches tend to avoid saying it outright. Personnel managers often soften the blow by talking about the varied abilities in every human being which may pass through the net of examinations, etc. etc. More finely, as in some finance firms in London, judgments of potential ability tend to be informal, senior management acting on gut feeling about their juniors' potential as much as on the objective trading record; year-end bonuses may be awarded in ways which resemble the ancient Roman practice of divining the future from the entrails of dead animals. The sting of being left behind, of being unrewarded, is stronger in these firms than in investment banks, where either the bonus or future prospects are simply calculated by the trading record.

The untalented become invisible, they simply drop from view in institutions covertly judging ability rather than achievement. Here again organizations mirror what people may have experienced earlier in life at school. Youngsters judged to be without talent do not stand out as distinctive individuals, they become a collective body, a mass. Meritocracy, as Young understood, is a system as well as an idea, a system based on institutional indifference once a person is judged.[14] The problem is compounded, as Gardner has shown, just because the talent searches do not try to cast a wide net, paralleling the diverse kinds of abilities diverse individuals may possess; the search for potential ability is narrow-focus.

School and work differ in one crucial way about the process. Though in principle there should be nothing a student could do about his or her innate ability, in well-known fact it is possible with sufficient tutoring to raise scores significantly in retaking the tests. In the work world, on the contrary, there are seldom second chances. In flexible organizations, employee records constitute the one hard possession of the firm. In studying one set of such records, I was struck by how little revision the personnel manager had made over time to individual case files; the first judgments instead set the standard, later entries sought for consistency; translation of the records into numeric form usable by core managers only made the documents more rigid in content.

The belief of many workers let go or held back in work that they have been judged unfairly illustrates another dimension of judgmental power, one which again does not fit into Foucault's scheme. Those who are discarded are often correct interpreters of their experience: they have not indeed been judged fairly, on the basis of their achievements. The sense of being unfairly judged comes from the ways in which firms themselves are run. To understand why, we might recall some of the idealized traits of a worker in the cutting-edge institution.

An organization in which the contents are constantly shifting requires the mobile capacity to solve problems; getting deeply involved in any one problem would be dysfunctional, since projects end as abruptly as they begin. The problem analyzer who can move on, whose product is possibility, seems more attuned to the instabilities which rule the global marketplace. The social skill required by a flexible organization is the ability to work well with others in short-lived teams, others you won't have the time to know well. Whenever the team dissolves and you enter a new group, the problem you have to solve is getting down to business as quickly as possible with these new teammates. "I can work with anyone" is the social formula for potential ability. It won't matter who the other person is; in fast-changing firms it can't matter. Your skill lies in cooperating, whatever the circumstances.

These qualities of the ideal self are a source of anxiety because *disempowering* to the mass of workers. As we have seen, in the workplace they produce social deficits of loyalty and informal trust, they erode the value of accumulated experience. To which we should now add the hollowing out of ability.

A key aspect of craftsmanship is learning how to get something right. Trial and error occurs in improving even seemingly routine tasks; the worker has to be free to make mistakes, then go over the work again and again. Whatever a person's innate abilities, that is, skill develops only in stages, in fits and starts—in music, for instance, even the child prodigy will become a mature artist only by occasionally getting things wrong and learning from mistakes. In a speeded-up institution, however, time-intensive learning becomes difficult. The pressures to produce results quickly are too intense; as in educational testing, so in the workplace time-anxiety causes people to skim rather than to dwell. Such hollowing out of ability compounds the organizations' tendency to discount past achievement in looking toward the future.

When people have spoken to me about not being able to show what they can do, I've sensed they are referring to just this sense of being prevented from developing their skills. When I interviewed back-office workers in a health maintenance organization, for instance, they complained that the time pressures meant they did a "middling" job of making sense of the accounts; people who worked quickly were rewarded with promotion, but the bills they processed proved frequently a muddle on closer inspection. In call centers, management similarly frowns on employees who spend too much time on the telephone—too responsive, for instance, to fuddled customers who can't express themselves clearly. Anyone who has spent time at a budget-airline ticket counter knows the problem: impatience is institutionalized.

In principle, any well-run firm should want its employees to learn from their mistakes and admit a certain degree of trial-and-error learning. In practice, such big firms do not. The size of the firm indeed makes the greatest difference in this regard: in small service firms (under a hundred or so employees) care of customers is more directly connected to the firms' survival. But in the large medical insurance company superficiality proved functional; taking too much time to straighten things out earned no rewards. The result, within the firms I and my colleagues studied—perhaps invisible to a frustrated customer—was a fair number of employees who also feel frustrated.

• • •

In sum, the material specter of uselessness lifts the curtain on a fraught cultural drama. How can one become valuable and useful in the eyes of others? The classic way in which people do so is the craftsman's way, by developing some special talent, some particular skill. The claims of craftsmanship are challenged in modern culture by an alternative formula of value.

In its origin, meritocracy sought to offer opportunity to individuals with exceptional ability—Jefferson's "natural aristocracy." It took on an ethical cast in arguing that such people deserved opportunity; it was a matter of justice that society provide for them. In the beginning, this search pitted one elite against another, the natural aristocracy against inherited privilege. In the course of time society has refined the technology of searching for unusual talent. In prospecting for the potential to grow rather than for past achievement, the search for talent well suits the peculiar conditions of flexible organizations. These organizations use the same instruments for a larger purpose: to eliminate as well as promote individuals. The invidious comparisons between people become deeply personal. In this talent cull, those judged without inner resources are left in limbo. They can be judged no longer useful or valuable, despite what they have accomplished.

CHAPTER THREE

Consuming Politics

I s the new economy breeding a new politics? In the past, inequality furnished the economic energy for politics; today inequality is being reconfigured both in terms of raw wealth and work experience.

The generation of great wealth at the very top of the social order is notorious; more largely consequent may be the class divide between those who profit from the new economy and those in the middle who do not: the labor analyst Robert Reich speaks, for instance, of a "two-tier" society in which the "skills elite," the "masters of information," and the "symbolic analysts" cleave away from a stagnant middle class.[1]

At the bottom, Alain Touraine points out, a class difference appears between those laborers—mostly immigrants in the informal, or "gray," sectors of the economy—who find room for themselves in a fluid or fragmented economy and those traditional working-class people, once protected by pyramidal unions or employers, who have less room for maneuver. In the middle, people fear being displaced, sidelined, or under-used. The institutional model of the future does not furnish them a life narrative at work, or the promise of much security in the public realm. In the network society, their informal networks are thin.

In the age of social capitalism, strains on the economic system produced *ressentiment.* The word names a cluster of emotions, principally the belief that ordinary people who have played by the rules have not been dealt with fairly. Ressentiment is an intensely social emotion which tends to stray from its economic origins—it produces resentment at being patronized by the elite, or anger at Jews or other internal enemies who seem to steal social prizes to which they have no right. In the past, under the sway of ressentiment, religion and patriotism became weapons of revenge. This emotion has not disappeared. In the United States today, ressentiment may explain why so many workers once center-left have moved far to the right, translating material stress into cultural symbols.

While real, ressentiment seems to me too narrow a way to relate economics and politics because material insecurity prompts more than ways to demonize those who herald unsettling change. The economy is also a teacher: We might get deeper into people's everyday experience by exploring the distinctive ways in which people learn how to consume the new—new goods and services—and then ask ourselves, Do people indeed shop for politicians the way they shop for clothes? Rather than just as an angry voter, we might want to consider the citizen as a consumer of politics, faced with pressures to buy.

The matter of consumption takes us into the heart of the new economy, and particularly onto the floor of the giant firm Wal-Mart. This global, cut-price retailer employed 1.4 million workers worldwide in 2004; its revenues of $258 billion "are 2 percent of US GDP and eight times the size of Microsoft's."[2] This new company has innovated in its suppliers, drawing on fast-developing Chinese manufacturing, and in its uses of advanced technology. The McKinsey Institute names Wal-Mart as the very acme of a cutting-edge firm, its productivity coming from an "ongoing managerial innovation" which has concentrated power at the center of the giant, has disempowered unions, and has dealt with its mass of workers as though they were provisional, temporary laborers.[3]

The appeal of this megalith to consumers is that everything they might want to buy cheap—clothes, auto goods, food, perfume, computers, . . .—is in one place. The centralization of command seems mirrored in the position of a consumer wandering the aisles of a Wal-Mart, everything available instantly, the clothes only a few steps away from the computers. Though its employees are, in my experience, mostly helpful, as a class the salesperson has been in Wal-Mart stripped out of the consumption process: there's no face-to-face mediation and persuasion here. In this the firm resembles other cutting-edge bureaucracies which have stripped out their middle, interpretative layers of staff. The decision about which cut-price product to buy turns on global imaging and marketing.

Absurd as it may seem, we might refine the question about economics and politics to this: Do people shop for politicians the way they shop at Wal-Mart?

That is, has the centralized grip of political organizations grown greater at the expense of local, mediating party politics? Has the merchandizing of political leaders come to resemble that of selling soap, as instantly recognizable brands which the political consumer chooses off the shelf?

If we answer yes to all of the above, the crux of politics becomes marketing, which seems bad for political life. The very idea of democracy requires mediation and face-to-face discussion; it requires deliberation rather than packaging. Following this train of thought, we would observe with dismay that all the seductive tricks of advertising are now deployed to market the personalities and ideas of politicians; more finely, just as advertising seldom makes things difficult for the customer, so the politician makes him or herself easy to buy.

This obvious answer I want to dispute. Not that it's wrong, but that the new economy makes both marketing and politics more complicated. Wal-Mart has certainly oppressed its workers but serves a real need for its customers.[4] Only a snob could look down on cheap products; should we then look down on "cheap" politics? The political version of the megastore could repress local democracy but enable, as advertising does, individual fantasy; erode the content and substance of politics but stimulate the imagination for change.

Political rectitude will treat this simply as a frivolous thought. The avatars of the new capitalism have, however, argued forcefully that the new structures mobilize the imagination of change. We need at least to keep an open mind about how politicians now become marketed, and the institutions which market them— the effort of keeping an open mind on this subject, I must admit, is difficult for me, since the loss of local, mediating politics seems to me indeed a fatal wound. If the economy continues to move toward the cutting-edge model, however, and political ideals remain backward looking, then the ideal becomes no more than an impotent regret.

The Self-Consuming Passion

The ancient Athenians separated the place where they did politics, the Pnyx, from the central economic space of the city, the Agora. The separation embodies a classic proposition in social thought, that economic activity enervates people's capacity for politics. The logic is simple: to Plato it appeared that economics operates on need and greed, while politics should operate on justice and right. Closer to modern times, separating economics and politics took a different twist, as Albert Hirschman has documented in *The Passions and the Interests*; trading appeared in the sixteenth and seventeenth centuries to be a more peaceable and moderate activity than politics, whose real passions tended to violence.[5]

The belief that economics saps the energy needed for politics reappeared in the industrial era, in some versions of Marxism. Now, it was argued, the physical deprivations and soul-destroying rigors of factory labor focused workers simply on survival, leaving no mental room to reimagine a different form of collective life. A revolutionary vanguard would have to do that thinking for them. The political imagination, that is, requires a certain measure of protection from economic experience. Today this classic, negative proposition has taken another turn, one that more concerns everyday life than theory, due to the meaning of consumption itself.

In poetic usage, a consuming passion can connote a passion that burns itself out by its own intensity; put in less lurid form, in using things we use them up. Our desire for a dress may be ardent, but a few days after we actually buy and wear it, the garment arouses us less. Here the imagination is strongest in anticipation, grows ever weaker through use. Today's economy strengthens this kind of self-consuming passion, both in shopping malls and in politics.

Honoré de Balzac was the great nineteenth-century artist of self-consuming passions. His characters, so ardent in wanting what they don't have, lose their ardor once possessed. These characters are forerunners of Proust's famous Erotic Law, that the more inaccessible someone is, the more we desire him. In *Le Père Goriot*, Balzac imagines this psychology to embody a social transition, a shift from old-fashioned peasants clinging to everything they have accumulated to more cosmopolitan characters who dwell in material desires which die when consummated. The sociologist might explain this social shift as a change in institutions, such as the weakening of inherited lands or houses as a basis for wealth, or the swelling of disposable, salaried income which could be more freely and regularly spent, or again the cornucopia of new things to buy machine production made possible.

Surfeit and waste are married in the self-consuming passion. Were we able to peek into the wardrobe of a

Parisian clerk's home in the ancien regime, for instance, we would find only a few women's dresses, perhaps two sets of male clothes, and shoes handed down across the generations—all made by hand. In the kitchen we would find a single set of dishes, a few pots, spoons, and ladles, again all made by hand. In Balzac's time, mechanical production both reduced the cost and increased the volume of such ordinary goods. Only by the mid–nineteenth century was it possible for a family of modest means to contemplate throwing out worn shoes rather than mending them, or to possess a battery of clothes adapted to the seasons. Mechanical production explains Georg Lukac's observation that Balzac was a prophet of capitalism's expansion of desire, but the cornucopia in itself does not explain the subsequent withering of pleasure in possession.

In the twentieth century two explanations were advanced for the self-consuming passion, neither entirely satisfactory. One was the "motor of fashion," which means that advertising and the mass media learned how to mold desires so that people feel dissatisfied with the things they have; this was the view influentially put forward by Vance Packard in his mid-century study *The Hidden Persuaders*.[6] Here market-

ing is the evil. The other explanation was "planned obsolescence," which argued that things were built not to
last, in order that the public would buy new things. The
facts on which this latter explanation drew came from
the American auto and clothing industries, the cars so
poorly welded, the clothes so poorly stitched that they
became junk after two or three years.[7] Here production
is the evil.

While there is merit in both views, both assume
the consumer to play a passive role—as the mere play-
thing of advertising or the prisoner of junk. Yet changes
in work and the search for talent show how individuals
could be more actively involved in the self-consuming
passion.

The change in work bureaucracies, probed in
chapter 1, showed the fragility of a person's hold over a
place in a cutting-edge institution. Work is not a possession, nor does it have a fixed content, but becomes
instead a position in a constantly changing network. A
network node—that curiously content-free word used
in management-speak—differs from an office in Max
Weber's sense. People may jockey fiercely for position
in the corporation, but not to possess any one location
as an end in itself. As the first chapter tried to make

clear, this experience is larger than simply being so ambitious one is never content with what one has. Work identities get used up, they become exhausted, when institutions themselves are continually reinvented. Much corporate restructuring has similarly the character of a self-consuming passion at work, most notably in the pursuit of prospective "synergies" when firms are combined. Once the marriage is effected and staff is cut, the pursuit of synergy wanes. This was the case, for instance, in the merger of Time Warner and AOL in the late 1990s, a desire which faded once it became possible to enact.

The modern frame gives talent a cast which is akin to the self-consuming passion. In chapter 2, we saw how fixed skills are rapidly challenged in the advanced sectors of technology, medicine, and finance. The value placed on craftsmanship, doing something for its own sake, sits ever more uneasily in institutions where process and networking rule. Instead, the flexible organization puts a premium on portable human skills, on being able to work on several problems with a shifting cast of characters, cutting loose action from context. The search for talent, in particular, focuses on people with a talent for problem solving no matter the context, a talent which skirts becoming too ingrown. Potential ability emphasizes the prospect of doing things one has yet to do; achievement and mastery are self-consuming, the contexts and contents of knowledge used up in being used.

Consumption of goods plays a key role in complementing and legitimating these experiences. When people come to buy things, marketing the self-consuming passion seem *desirable*. It does so in two ways, one straightforward, the other subtle; the straightforward way occurs through branding, the subtle way through investing things to buy with potency and potential.

Branding and Potency

In a study of consumer desire, Sharon Zukin has framed the practical dilemma of shopping thus: "The consumer lacks the production knowledge that earlier generations commanded." Specifically, "by the Sixties, Americans no longer knew how to milk a cow, make a bagel, or build a car out of a soapbox or a packing crate."[8] This meant to Zukin that the person trying to buy intelligently needs a new understanding of physical things:

"instead of production knowledge ... craft knowledge," by which Zukin means "a sensory appreciation
of a product's qualities, a modest understanding of different production techniques, and the imagination to
construct a product's 'back story'—a social narrative of
the cultural tradition from which the product comes."[9]
In other words, the modern consumer needs to think
like a craftsman without being able to do what a craftsman does.

Ideally, this should be true. And, in practice, one
virtue of Wal-Mart, particularly in its in-house products,
lies in the utilitarian character of its stores—those endless rows of shelves stacked high with things the consumer has to know something about in order to select.
Other ways of marketing, however, seek to prevent consumers from thinking like craftsmen about a product's
utility. Instead, branding seeks to make a basic product
sold globally seem distinctive, seeks to obscure homo-
geneity. The means of doing so today are more complicated than Packard's concept of the "motor of fashion."

Today, manufacturing deploys on a global scale
the "platform construction" of goods from automo-
biles to computers to clothes. The platform consists of
a basic object on which minor, surface changes are im-

posed in order to convert the product into a particular brand. The production process is not quite the familiar industrial one of mass-produced goods. Modern technologies can quickly transform the shape and size of bottles or boxes; the contents can also be redecorated more quickly in electronic production than on the old-fashioned assembly line, in which tools were made fit for a single purpose.

Manufacturers call these changes built on the modern platform gold-plating, and that image is exact. To sell a basically standardized thing, the seller will magnify the value of minor differences quickly and easily engineered, so that the surface is what counts. The brand must seem to the consumer more than the thing itself.

Automobile manufacture is a good example. Giant firms like Volkswagen and Ford can and do produce versions of a global automobile—a basic platform of frame, engine, and body parts—then gold-plate surface differences. Often, in this kind of production, the rough assembly work on the platform will occur in low-wage countries in the developing world; the gold-plating will occur in finishing plants closer to local markets. Computers come into being in the same way:

the chips, circuit boards, and faces produced on a common platform far from the market become a brand near to markets in both place and time.

The problem for the platform manufacturer is how to make differentiation profitable. Chimpanzees and human beings share about 96 percent of the same genetic DNA. The Volkswagen corporation has to convince consumers that the differences between a modest Skoda and a top-end Audi—which share about 90 percent of their industrial DNA—justify selling the top model for more than twice the low-end model. How can a 10 percent difference in content be inflated into a 100 percent difference in price? The problem can be equally framed in terms of services: An airplane's speed could be considered its service platform. The average business-class ticket on a trans-Atlantic flight costs four to five times an economy fare, but the businessman gets nothing like four to five times the space or service—and the speed remains the same in all cabins. Again, neither Skodas nor Audis tend to wear out quickly; their platforms are of excellent quality. This admirable manufacturing fact poses an economic threat. Were the company to emphasize the virtues of sheer utility and possession, it would sell fewer cars, and craftsman-buyers in Zukin's sense would tend to be Skoda-minded.

Imaging difference thus becomes all-important in producing profits. If differences can be magnified in a certain way, the viewer will experience the consuming passion.

In British advertising, the Skoda is presented as a thing in itself, the car shown clearly inside and out, often with lots of informative print to round out the presentation. The high-end Audi, by contrast, tends to give a view from the driver's seat, looking out. The ads have little text, and the view changes from advert to advert, depending on whether the high-end model is an open-top coupe or a sedan equally at home in the Sahara and the shopping mall. The visual difference aims to destroy any association in the buyer's mind between Skoda and Audi.

By diminishing attention to what the object is, the manufacturer hopes to sell its associations; by constantly altering the view out the window, the manufacturer hopes to emphasize the "driving experience," a process which changes constantly, seeming to offer in different brands and models a different view out of the car window. Of course in functional terms this is the equivalent of saying that business-class passenger fly faster across the Atlantic than people in the back of the airplane. The challenge of all branding is to create variations of that illusory theme by decontextualizing.

Gold-plating has changed the terms of planned obsolescence as these were framed a half century ago. When W. Edwards Deming advanced his ideas for total-quality management, he faced a productive reality in which defective products were accepted by consumers as normal—rather like the situation today in which consumers accept as normal the poor initial quality of new software. The Japanese auto and electronic manufacturers who responded to Deming's ideas sought to create products which did not become obsolete on purpose, and so create a new market niche. Firms like Toyota and Sony succeeded brilliantly in doing so. Their machines were "fit-for-purpose," in Deming's phrase, which has the double meaning of a machine doing just what it should do and doing it robustly, the way an athlete is fit. Automated production and electronic product surveillance have since enabled total-quality management to become today's normal.

The problem is of course that once this high standard is reached, the demand for a product trails off. This challenge is in one way not new. When Henry Ford declared in the 1920s that the customer could have any Model T car he or she liked so long as it was black, his son Edsel Ford riposted that colors make profits. What's changed now is the participation of the consumer in the process of magnifying differences. Here we pass from what marketing intends to why consumers respond.

The consumer seeks the stimulation of difference from goods which are increasingly homogenized. He or she resembles a tourist who travels from one clone city to the next, visiting the same shops, buying the same products in each. But he or she has traveled: for the consumer, stimulation lies in the very process of moving on. The sociologist Guy Debord thought this is what a consumer does *to* things—changing one's desire becomes, like traveling, a kind of spectacle; it doesn't matter that the things one buys remain the same so long as one can sense oneself shifting.[10] The sociologist Erving Goffman, in his last studies of advertising, took a complimentary view of the consumer's involvement. He emphasized that the most sophisticated forms of publicity are "half finished frames" which invite the consumer to participate by filling in the picture.[11] Ironic adverts do this; so does selling a car by showing the Sahara but no car. The result is the same for Debord and Goffman. The consumer is engaged by his or her own mobility and imagination: Movement and incompleteness equally energize the imagination; fixity and solidity equally deaden it. The consumer participates in the act of branding, and in this act, it is the gold-plate rather than the platform which matters.

As a rather Skoda-minded soul, I had difficulty taking such views seriously, until I sat in on a set of product conferences about vodka at an advertising agency in New York. The elemental fact about vodka is that it has no taste and virtually no smell. For several weeks I witnessed the "creative team" at the agency agonize about how to sell a new brand of this anonymous alcohol; the solution they came up with consisted in pictures of sexy male and female midriffs joined with the name of the product, without any indication of what kind of product this was. The consumer was meant to do all the work of association. The genius of the campaign, evidently, is that the naked midriff images would change from month to month, thus producing what one person explained to me as "compound associational effects." (Few of the creative team, I might note, actually drank hard liquor.)

Though advertising which invites imaginative participation is hardly unique to modern times, it has a specific weight today. For example, Marx's dictum "all that is solid melts into air" was balanced, in the opening pages of *Kapital*, by a quite different analysis of commodity fetishism. To Marx, mundane things invested so magically with human meanings dwelt in a kind of personal museum, one in which the consumer added more and more to his collection; the consumer hoarded his treasures, his aim was accumulation. The last thing the consumer wanted was to give up these fetishes into which he had invested so much of himself. Now, in the kind of consumption described by Debord and Goffman, surrender of an object is not experienced as loss. Rather abandonment fits into the process of finding new stimulations—the objects particularly easy to give up since they are basically standardized goods.

Thus the self-consuming passion appears. Should we sneer at this invitation to fantasize? The strict utilitarian would do so, preferring to live in a Skoda-functional world. The true craftsman might not care, so long as the goods are good. But freedom from possessiveness is also a kind of freedom. To look ahead, mightn't it be better for citizens to vote for what might be, for a shared imagination, rather than vote to defend their particular interests, to protect what they already possess?

• • •

A second sign of the consuming passion lies in potency. Potency is something we can buy—here I'm thinking about machines rather than sex pills. A commonplace in the electronics industry is that ordinary consumers buy equipment whose capabilities they will never use: memory hard-drives which can store four hundred books, though most people will store at best a few hundred pages of letters, or software programs which sit unopened on the computer. The behavior of these punters parallels that of the buyers of super-fast sports cars who mostly crawl in bumper-to-bumper traffic, or of the owners of the infamous SUV machines meant for desert navigation used mostly to shepherd children to and from school. These are all consumers of potency.

From the origins of capital markets, investors have been driven by irrational belief in the power of objects, as in the "tulip mania" of English investors in the seventeenth century, when trade in these prosaic, useless bulbs promised somehow to make British bankers rich—a precursor of the dot.com investment madness of the 1990s. The attraction in this kind of consumption is that capital will increase through the investor's exploiting of possibilities unforeseen by others, or through sheer magic. Buying a potent machine has another kind of appeal, embodied in one small, beautiful object currently on the market.

This is the iPod, capable of storing and playing ten thousand three-minute songs. How, though, would you go about choosing the ten thousand songs, or find the time to download them? What will be your principles for sorting out the five hundred hours of music contained in the little white box? Could you possibly remember the ten thousand songs in order to choose which one you wanted to hear at any given moment? (This human memory feat would entail, in classical music, the ability to know by heart virtually all the compositions of Johann Sebastian Bach.)

Scholars in the Renaissance learned to memorize an immense amount of factual material by imagining themselves in a theater: they would group facts into categories represented by a character on stage like Apollo, standing for astronomy, and Neptune, representing navigation; the mental spectator then invented a story woven around Apollo and Neptune in order to correlate the varied facts contained in the two realms.[12]

This kind of memory theater is not built into the random-access procedures of an iPod. The written bumpf which accompanies the iPod admits as much. The machine is "content neutral;" the bumpf suggests visiting various Internet sites with protocols for downloading material, but visits reveal only further neutrality. One site, for instance, offers three thousand golden oldies, after which follows an alphabetic enumeration of each of the three thousand titles. But again there is the difficulty of hearing nine thousand minutes in the mind. Not surprisingly, Michael Bull, who has written a study of how people use the Walkman, the iPod's primitive parent, has found that people listened to the same twenty or thirty songs over and over again— which is as much active musical memory as most people possess.[13]

Yet the iPod's phenomenal commercial appeal consists precisely in having more than a person could ever use. Part of the appeal lies in a connection between material potency and one's own potential ability. The talent searcher, we have seen, is less interested in what you already know, more in how much you might be able to learn; the personnel director is less interested in what you already do than in who you might become. Buying a little iPod similarly promises to expand one's capabilities; all machines of this sort trade on the buyer's identification with the overloaded capacity built into the machines. The machine becomes like a giant medical prosthesis. If the iPod is potent, but the user cannot master that potency, the machines have great appeal, then, just for that reason. As the salesman who flogged my iPod said, without any embarrassment, "The sky's the limit." I bought.

Put abstractly: desire becomes mobilized when potency is divorced from practice; put simply: you don't limit what you want to what you can do. In a way the Wal-Mart also epitomizes this divorce, a vast assembly under one roof of more than any one person could buy; the sheer mass of the objects stimulates desire. There is a contrast in this between the Wal-Mart and the first department stores, which appeared in Paris in the late nineteenth century. In those commercial emporiums, marketing consisted in displaying a group of dissimilar objects, one or two of each, in a single setting; for instance, a saucepan might be laid on a Persian carpet, next to a bottle of expensive perfume. The merchandiser meant to stimulate the buyer by making the ordinary strange, whereas, in the Wal-Mart, it is the sheer number and excess of objects which stimulate.

• • •

In sum, the consuming passion takes two forms: active engagement in imaging and arousal by potency. The consumer who enters the marketing game of imaging can lose a sense of proportion, mistaking the gold-plating instead of its platform as an object's real value. So does the celebration of potency pose risks—to firms as well as to individuals. In the era of American trusts and monopolies, magnates like Carnegie and Rockefeller sought to foreclose on the unruly dynamism of markets because they wanted submission from smaller suppliers and distributors rather than competitors enacting the entrepreneurial fantasy of becoming Rockefellers themselves. Similar in intent was Bismarck's determination to create solid bureaucracies: if workers

and soldiers felt themselves filled with all sorts of un-
tapped, undefined possibilities they might no longer be
obedient. Today, in cutting-edge organizations, the ide-
ology of potency can suggest to management future
possibilities greater than the institution's present grasp;
in pursuit of that goal management can become more
centralizing and directive, employees in turn losing out
or, as in the BBC, no longer certain about how to survive.

The ethos of potency can make companies themselves vulnerable, as when investors see in them some in-
definable possibility for growth. The history of mergers
and acquisitions is littered with firms like the Sunbeam
Corporation, which did very well producing prosaic domestic appliances until a small group of rich investors
decided it could be remade to become a much more
important firm; this siren appeal nearly shipwrecked
the company. The firm, then, can behave like a consumer who submits to the consuming passion, casting
aside things which work well.

But still, the machines I've described—iPods,
SUVs, computers filled with a cornucopia of software
programs—do make a positive appeal to the imagination. So does a megastore like Wal-Mart. The Puritan
dwells in suspicion; we want instead pleasure. What

I've described are pleasures which consumers *make* in things, imposed pleasure which a sober utilitarian would and doubtless should suspect. And the declaration that "the sky's the limit" could be defended on political grounds: people might be set free by dreaming of something beyond the routines and confines of everyday life. In the same way they might be set free by feeling they've used up and exhausted these perfectly workable ways of getting by. Aren't people set free when they transcend in spirit what they directly know, use, or need? The consuming passion might be another name for liberty.

At least that's the proposition I now want to explore.

Citizen as Consumer

I began thinking about this connection, circuitously, when visiting two cutting-edge research laboratories, Xerox Park in Silicon Valley and the Media Lab at MIT. Both are premised on the idea that puritan utility cramps the spirit of innovation, both have played with vague scientific possibilities rather than adhered to mechanistic models of research, both have produced immensely puissant, practical results inadvertently by chance. Xerox Park stumbled on the computer screen icon, the Media Lab on a host of software programs. Though I little understand their scientific labors, both places struck me as somehow democratic.

That impression is strengthened by the view Hannah Arendt put forward in her writings on the democratic process.[14] For her, the "policy wonk," that technician of power, is the citizen's enemy. In a truly democratic forum, every citizen should have the right to think aloud and debate with others, no matter if he or she is not an expert. Nor should the test of utility and practicality rule: this test emphasizes what is rather than what might be. Arendt wants to give the political imagination free play, in something like the experimental spirit of the Media Lab.

More, Arendt subscribes to her own version of the consuming passion: citizens make laws, live with them, use them up, and then give birth to something new, even though the old law might still prove mechanically viable. Here her thinking is quite precise: she takes aim against the jurist's insistence on precedent, contests the deadening weight of case law, subscribes to a peculiar vision of common law which gives more room for innovation. The dramatization of potential appears in Arendt's late writings on collective will; like Arthur Schopenhauer, she came to believe that the strength of will taps into sources which lie beyond representations and transcriptions of things in everyday life.[15]

These views look backward to Jefferson's democratic ideal, in which citizens rebel every two generations against the deadening weight of the past, and forward to visions like that of the social philosopher Ulrich Beck, in whose "risk society" people are willing to take chances without knowing what will result. [16]

In practice, of course, a political figure who cuts loose from hard facts can be merely an opportunist. But the cynic is often left behind by political reality. This was the case of the movement for black civil rights in America, energized at a key moment of protest by Martin Luther King's speech "I Have a Dream," delivered at the height of the search for justice. Derided by realists in the press and in government, he moved a mass of listeners forward to action. The language he used deployed the rhetoric of personal potential and the surrender of past, routinized habits of racial separation. King was the perfect Arendtian. The pursuit of justice was for him more than a set of policy fixes; it required a fresh page.

We might expect a culture like ours, with so little possessive regret, so attuned to change, to strengthen the progressive prospect. In this best-case scenario, the time of possession would shorten, as in the labor process. The political public would expand to global dimensions, as in the investment process. There have indeed been moments in the past decade when, interviewing some managers of cutting-edge businesses, I've been almost convinced that new economic conditions might produce a progressive politics. These are younger business leaders who made fortunes in technology and are now ploughing money back into civil society, particularly into environmental causes and work retraining schemes. They believe that the new ideal of selfhood in business is a model for the empowered citizen, as the citizen imagined in social capitalism was not: proactive rather than submissive.

Yet their dream, I have come to think, is ill-founded. To explain why the new institutions will not produce a progressive politics, I want to focus on something which consumption and politics share— theater.

The realm of consumption is theatrical because the seller, like a playwright, has to command the willing suspension of disbelief in order for the consumer to buy. Even the prosaic Wal-Mart is such a theater, in which the size and sheer mass of goods on offer change the spectator-consumer's understanding of the things in themselves. Today, the consuming passion has a dramatic power: possessive use is less arousing to the spectator-consumer than the desire for things he does not yet have; the dramatization of potential leads the spectator-consumer to desire things he cannot fully use.

Politics is equally theatrical, and progressive politics in particular requires a certain kind of rhetoric. It deploys a willing suspension of disbelief of citizens in their own accumulated experience. I've tried to accent the positive side of this. But, like the marketing of consumer goods, the marketing of politics can take a much more negative turn. What's missing in the hope for progressive change is an understanding of the profoundly *enervating* role that illusion plays in modern society. I mean here to propound a paradox, that people can actively enter into their own passivity.

I'll address five ways in which the consumer-spectator-citizen is turned away from progressive politics and toward this more passive state. The list is hardly exhaustive, but each element arises directly from the culture of the new capitalism portrayed in these pages. To guide the reader, here's the list of five: the consumer-spectator-citizen is (1) offered political platforms which resemble product platforms and (2) gold-plated differences; (3) asked to discount "the twisted timber of humanity" (as Immanuel Kant called us) and (4) credit more user-friendly politics; (5) accept continually new political products on offer.

The political platform: The VW platform is a common chassis from which small material differences are inflated in value to become brands. Modern politics has a similar form, which we commonly call consensus politics. In Britain today, for example, New Labour and modern Toryism share a pretty-much standard platform: business-friendly, socially inclusive, immigrant-ambivalent. Platform politics operated in this way for most of the latter half of the twentieth century in the United States, up to the era of the second president George Bush. The Republican and Democratic parties sounded very different but behaved in office very much the same; President Ronald Reagan, supposedly hard right, expanded the bureaucracy of central government, ran up Keynesian-size deficits, and successfully pursued detente with the Soviet empire, while President Bill Clinton nurtured business, resisted elevation of the minimum wage, and vigorously made small-scale war. The only practicing Arendtians for many decades were the courts, in their rulings on racial segregation, abortion, crime, housing, and corporate accountability; today their transforming work remains the target of the second Bush regime.[17]

What the simple label of consensus politics doesn't explain is the forces driving politics onto a common ground. Today, European political scientists have labeled the United States and the United Kingdom neoliberal regimes to indicate that in both nations a centrist political platform enabled economic development friendly to globalization, flexibility, and meritocracy. These forces are hardly unique, though, to the Anglo-American sphere. They represent a logical progression in other societies moving beyond the confines social capitalism.

The single most important common element in this platform is the state's role. Far from becoming weaker, the state remains strongly directive. The center controls infusion of resources into devolved institutions and monitors performance. It does not lead, in the Weberian sense: power and authority instead divide. As in business, so in politics bureaucracies increasingly centralize power while refusing to take responsibility for their citizens. This divorce between power and authority—analyzed in the first chapter as a business phenomenon—is anything but politically progressive.

By *progressive* I mean here that a good polity is one in which all citizens believe they are bound together in a common project. Social capitalism created that common project through civic institutions based on a military model; the vice of social capitalism was the iron cage of solidarity. The new institutional order eschews responsibility, labeling its own indifference as freedom for individuals or groups on the periphery; the vice of the politics derived from the new capitalism is indifference.

Gold-plating: As the state assumes this new platform, the rhetoric of competing political parties necessarily has to stress differences. Indeed, by concentrating on the platform alone as reality, we would miss the lived experience of political life, which is that differences are what really arouse voters and the media. Gold-plating explains how this arousal occurs. The simplest form of political gold-plating is symbol inflation. In Britain, the parties have differed passionately on whether or not hunting foxes with dogs ought to be allowed; approximately seven hundred hours of Parliamentary time were recently allotted to this issue, whereas the creation of a Supreme Court for the United Kingdom was debated for eighteen hours. There's nothing new in symbolic inflation of trivia—what is new is the consonance between the advertising of products and political behavior. The marketing of political personalities comes increasingly to resemble the marketing of soap in that the gold-plating of small differences is what the advertisers hope will grab the public's attention.

So familiar are we with this crossover from consumer to political behavior that we lose sight of the consequences: the press's and public's endless obsession with politicians' individual character traits masks the reality of the consensus platform. In modern political performances, the marketing of personality further and frequently eschews a narrative of the politician's history and record in office; it's too boring. He or she embodies intentions, desires, values, beliefs, tastes—an emphasis which has again the effect of divorcing power from responsibility.

Perhaps the most serious form of gold-plating in modern politics consists of recontextualizing fact. The advertisements for high-end autos, as we observed earlier in this chapter, as in the VW advertisements, make a brand out of a platformed product. In politics, the facts of immigration can be recontextualized and then marketed in just the same way. In Germany as in Britain, the bulk of immigrants are tax-paying workers, doing work cleaning hospitals and sweeping streets which native Brits and Germans eschew; to make political capital out of their presence, these necessary outsiders are repackaged so that they fit into the same box of culture as unproductive asylum seekers. In the United States, the branding of immigrants can be achieved in another way. Migrant workers, especially from Mexico, are tacitly accepted because, again, they're necessary to much of the American agricultural and service economy. They become political brands when repackaged culturally, as the political guru Samuel Huntington does in an influential recent book, *Who Are We?*[18] Mexicans loom as divided in loyalty between home and abroad, resistant to America's Protestant civic culture, as insidious colonizers from below. Like British foxes, Mexican-Americans are made to matter in ways larger than their behavior in picking grapes and sweeping the streets warrants.

Europe and North America for centuries have branded the Foreigner as a large, frightening presence, and today, as in the past, the Foreigner has become a symbolic site on which people can project all sorts of anxieties. The difference lies in what these anxieties are. Today, in addition to long-standing pure prejudice and political point scoring, experience of short-term, unstable bureaucracy shapes immigrant branding. In the labor realm, the Foreigner focuses anxieties about job loss or uselessness. Those anxieties make sense, as we've seen, when the foreigner is actually abroad, in an Indian call center or software firm; they make no sense projected onto an immigrant streetsweeper. Or rather, they make imaginative sense: the fear of loss of control now has a target close at hand. And in that perverse work of the imagination, it does not register that persecuting these close-by weak outsiders does little to make one's own job secure.

Platform and brand combine in politics to produce something other than a progressive desire for change—rather, a political climate akin to what Freud first called the "narcissism of small differences." As in advertising, so in politics branding can lead to loss of realistic, Skoda-minded judgment and opens a particularly modern door to prejudice.

The third reason the new order is not politically progressive lies in the consumer's conviction that whatever is, is not enough. Such a conviction operates in the economic sphere, as we have seen, when a profitable company is reorganized to make it grow; simply being profitable is not enough. A kindred way suspending present reality occurs in the search for talent, when the tester's focus shifts from actual achievement to a hypothetical capacity. Similarly in consumption: the gas-guzzling, monster SUVs which populate the American suburbs are machines dedicated to an imagined freedom; though stuck in traffic, one now has the potential to drive across a desert or through the Arctic.

Impatience with existing reality ought to be progressive. But the lesson politicians learn from cutting-edge institutions tends to be negative. The reason is that the sphere of everyday experience is slighted— the small, incremental losses and gains which make up the fabric of live experience. In the 1990s, for instance, a liberal-minded American government sought to reform the health care system, following the cutting-

edge model of treating health care as a series of transactions with doctors rather than long-term relationships. The reform ignored the dense, everyday experiences of patients and doctors in filling out forms; it
supposed well-organized computerized searches on the
Net could substitute for the time-consuming activity of
face-to-face diagnosis and treatment. The reformers
were impatient with the messy realities of being ill;
they instead treated the sick like entrepreneurs.

Impatience with "the twisted timber of humanity" has, of course, a long lineage—so long, indeed,
that policy making should have learned from it; policy
should grow from the ground up. In fact, the hold of
new institutional thinking, in politics and in business,
skirts doing so. Edmund Burke, Kant, and other ob-
servers of the French Revolution watched in horror
as the revolutionaries monitored and attacked the realities of everyday life, trying to straighten out the
twisted timber; the character of modern reform is instead uninterested; it neglects the ground because daily
life seems merely provisional.

My fourth worry is that when citizens act like
modern consumers they cease to think like craftsmen.
This worry complements the policymaker's inatten-

tion, but more finely; the citizen-as-consumer can disengage when political issues become difficult or resistant. The usual complaint about the media is that the worthy wooden master of policy bores and the glittering personality gains votes on the tube. The issue should instead be about how paying attention is oganized.

In labor, the good craftsman is more than a mechanical technician. He or she wants to understand why a piece of wood or computer code doesn't work; the problem becomes engaging and thereby generates objective attachment. This ideal comes to life in a traditional craft like making musical instruments; equally in a more modern setting like a scientific laboratory. And indeed in a well-run business: you don't want to run away from problems, you pay attention. But in consumption it's hard to think like a craftsman, as Zukin advocates. You buy because something is user-friendly, which usually means the user doesn't have to bother about how the thing, whether a computer or a car, works. The computer guru John Seely Brown reflects this divide between maker and consumer in arguing that the commercial challenge of modern electronic gadgets is to get "the technology out of the way"; the new machines should be as technically engaging and as easy to use as a telephone.

Of course no one wants to start the day reprogramming the computer. But user-friendly makes a hash of democracy. Democracy requires that citizens be willing to make some effort to find out how the world around them works. Few of the American proponents of the recent war in Iraq, for instance, wanted to learn about Iraq (most couldn't in fact locate Iraq on a map). Equally striking on the other side of the political spectrum, few proponents of stem-cell research have been curious about the arguments put forward by Catholic theologians against this research. The citizen-as-craftsman would make the effort in either case to find out; when democracy becomes modeled on consumption, becomes user-friendly, that will to know fades.

My point is not that people are lazy but that the economy creates a political climate in which citizens have difficulty in thinking like craftsmen. In institutions organized around flexible labor, getting involved deeply in something risks making the worker seem ingrown or narrowly focused. Again, in testing of ability, someone who becomes too curious about a specific problem will fail the test. Technology itself now works against engagement.

The iPod, I noted, disables its user by its very overcapacity; the glut of information generated by modern technology more largely threatens to make its receivers passive. Overload prompts disengagement. Seely Brown again makes a useful distinction in this regard between information and communication. An overwhelming volume of information, he suggests, is not an "innocent" problem; large amounts of raw data create a political fact: control becomes more centralized as volume increases.[19] Whereas in communication, the volume of information decreases as people interact and interpret; editing and elimination are the procedures which decentralize communication.

This may seem counterintuitive but makes sense if one thinks about communication in bureaucratic terms. As appeared in chapter 1, in the bureaucratic pyramid, information from the top is filtered, edited, and particularized as it passes down the chain of command; people communicate about the information. In the MP3 kind of institution, large bodies of data are centralized, ordered, and circulated in unalloyed form. Information remains intact on-screen as e-mail or numerical data. As the volume of this information in-creases—as it has done in the past generation—the receiver can react less to it, indeed disengages from it interpretatively. A text-message transaction, moreover, little resembles a conversation; its language is more primitive, and silences which register doubt or objec-tion, ironic gestures, momentary digressions—all the stuff of mutual communication—are eliminated in the technology. When rigorously institutionalized, the technology disables the craft of communication.

A last reason the modern political economy does not tend to progressive politics concerns trust. Robust empirical evidence backs up the cliché that people today have lost trust in politics and in politicians. Many politi-cians in turn blame the public for its cynicism. Beneath this mutual antagonism lies the question of *how* politi-cians earn trust; they cannot do so, I want to argue, by behaving like cutting-edge business executives.

To explain this, I ask the reader's forbearance for intruding my own experience with the British Labour Party. I moved to Britain just as Labour came to power, in 1997. For an entire generation before, Labour had struggled to shake off its socialist past; New Labour wanted to model itself on high-tech or advanced ser-

vice businesses, learning from their successes. I entered
this process informally in labor relations policy, since
I'd just finished a term presiding over the American
Council on Work, a loose organization of labor leaders,
academics, and businesspeople.

Once in power, New Labour began spinning out
policies for reform. The initial policies about work were
good: job training and counseling, industrial safety,
work-family issues all squarely addressed. Each year,
however, there were more policies, or different policies
which reformed the previous policies which reformed
the mess Labour had inherited. As the policies kept
coming, the public's trust in them eroded. Within the
councils of government, the manufacture of ever-new
policies appeared as an effort to learn from the actions
previously taken; to the public, the policy factory seemed
to indicate that government lacked commitment to any
particular course of action. At a meeting on the minimum wage, a union official glumly asked me, "What
happened to last year's policy?" The same process of
spewing out policy occurred in education and the health
services, with the same disenchanting effect. Even before the prime minister acted against the wishes of the

country in making war in Iraq, polls showed Labour had a severe problem of confidence.

Ironically, the only realm of New Labour policy which continued through its first eight years of power to command public trust lay in economic policy overseen by the Treasury, which was less fertile but more steady in its ideas. Ironic, because the manufacture of reform was so closely modeled on what government ministers saw as advanced business practices. As appeared in chapter 1, those practices breed anxiety—of a sort which the psychoanalyst Margaret Mahler once called "ontological insecurity." This label is not a piece of jargon; she aims to describe the fear of what will happen even if no disaster looms. Anxiety of this sort is also called free-floating to indicate that someone keeps worrying even if he or she has nothing to fear in a specific situation.

Labour invited this free-floating anxiety, even as its policies on the whole *were* working; as David Walker and Polly Toynbee have documented in some detail; over the course of its first eight years in power, New Labour steadily improved the lot of most Britons.[20] But to the public at large, again as measured by opinion polls, these real improvements were not reassuring. As a foreigner working in Britain, I was especially brought up short by a group of young unemployed workers being carefully retrained. Nothing comparable exists in the States, yet these young people couldn't connect the great care they were receiving with the government which made it possible; most said they were disappointed in Labour.

Britain under New Labour is, I well recognize, a special case. Most countries would beg for this kind of discontent. But I cite it just because the British state is indeed a progressive model. Yet ever fewer of its beneficiaries credit progress. The politicians I have worked with cited such reactions as "ungrateful"; critics in the media seize on them as due to the personalities of New Labour politicians, who are said to be "out of touch." It makes better sense to understand the problems politicians have encountered in terms of consumption. New Labour has behaved like consumers of policy, abandoning them as though they have no value once they exist. This consuming passion breaks trust in government: the public cannot credit that the policymaker ever believed in the policy he or she once put forward, then left behind.

In government policy, as in business, such a consumption mentality fits within the frame of new institutions. In both politics and business, short-term thinking prevails about *process;* slower, more sustained forms of growth are suspect. Sudden lurches of policy in business institutions produce ontological insecurity and free-floating anxiety; so too in public policy. People quite logically take their suspicions and unease about economic change into the political sphere, inferring that politicians are rudderless or lack commitment. When progressive politicians in particular think and behave like consumers, they can self-destruct, or produce the sour discontent which attends even the admirable policy reforms under way in Britain.

• • •

Here, then, are five reasons why on balance the new institutional model does not encourage progressive politics, even when its leaders intend to do good. Political science would probably identify the split between power and authority as the most consequent. To me, it seems that the culture of emerging institutional life plays an equally important role. The consuming passion fits into that culture, as does the meritocratic concept of talent and the idealized self which publicly eschews long-term dependency on others. These are cultural forms which celebrate personal change but not collective progress. The culture of the new capitalism is attuned to singular events, one-off transactions, interventions; to progress, a polity needs to draw on sustained relationships and accumulate experience. In short, the unprogressive drift of the new culture lies in its shaping of time.

Does this mean nothing can be done?

CHAPTER FOUR

Social Capitalism in Our Time

There were many foolish things about the New Left of my youth, fifty years ago, but in one way the movement was prescient beyond its years; the Port Huron Statement foresaw how state socialism could die from within. Socialism would suffocate under the weight of bureaucracy. Capitalism would remain, and remain the problem.

As I've sought to show in these pages, big bureaucracy can bind as well as oppress. This has long been true of armies; Max Weber witnessed how in his time economic and civil society institutions mimicked the social structure of armies, in pursuit of social inclusion and obedience to authority. The secret of this militarized capitalism lay in time—time structured so that people formed a life narrative and social relations within the institution. The price individuals paid for organized time could be freedom or individuality; the "iron cage" was both prison and home.

State socialism, as it developed in the Soviet empire after 1923, took on this military–capitalist legacy almost gladly. It thought the capitalist enemy lay in profits and markets rather than in bureaucracy. Like its enemy, the empire needed solidarity and subordination—bureaucracy became also the home and the prison of socialism. It was ironic that the New Left took aim in the 1960s at the military-capitalist-socialist behemoth because this was a decade of bureaucratic triumph, the factories of the Soviet empire finally becoming as productive economically as their brothers in the West. Looking back, the first sixty years of the twentieth century appear the age of the military machine, violent and self-destructive on the battlefield, triumphant, however, in the factory and the office. When the American president Dwight Eisenhower spoke of the "military-industrial complex," his image applied more broadly than to the manufacture of weapons.

The New Left hoped the behemoth would wither from within because it was a prison. Perversely, contemporary history has begun to grant that wish, though not in ways radicals of my youth would have wished. In the past three decades, bureaucracy has reorganized itself in the advanced economic sectors of global finance, technology, media, and merchandizing. This global spurt of growth may have brought many benefits, but a better quality of institutional life is not among them. The new institutions, as we have seen, are neither smaller nor more democratic; centralized power has instead been reconfigured, power split off from authority. The institutions inspire only weak loyalty, they diminish participation and mediation of commands, they breed low levels of informal trust and high levels of anxiety about uselessness. A shortened framework of institutional time lies at the heart of this social degradation; the cutting edge has capitalized on superficial human relations. This same shortened time framework has disoriented individuals in efforts to plan their life course strategically and dimmed the disciplinary power of the old work ethic based on delayed gratification.

This is a list of negatives. The positives invoked by these institutional changes are qualities of self which might allow individuals to flourish as institutional life becomes more shallow. These qualities are repudiation of dependence, development of one's potential ability, the capacity to transcend possessiveness. These qualities take us outside the realm of production, into the institutions of the welfare state, education, and consumption. The cutting edge of reform at work, as I have wanted to underline, is narrow; most people continue to labor under conditions Weber would well have understood. But the extension of the new values is broad. The positives invoked by the new order promise to consummate the project of meritocracy and to provide the model for progressive reform.

The remedy proposed by the New Left for the prison of bigness was cultural. Emotional declaration, made face to face, in small groups, would spawn a more humane order; the lessons of intimacy would be applied to society as a whole. Of course this scale is a young person's natural territory, and of course it cannot last; as adulthood unfolds, one's subjectivity becomes, if anything, more puzzling. And what the New Left might have learned from Bismarck, or from military service, is that strong social ties can flourish under quite impersonal conditions.

Yet I don't think the dreamers of my youth had the wrong idea in holding up material life to a cultural standard. As the reader may possibly have detected, I was one of those youthful dreamers. The normal path of the adult's "sentimental education" is meant to lead to ever greater resignation about how little life as it is actually conducted can accord with one's dreams. Ethnography about workers and their work has kept me off that path. The people I've interviewed, especially in the past decade, are too worried and disquieted, too little resigned to their own uncertain fate under the aegis of change. What they need most is a mental and emotional anchor; they need values which assess whether changes in work, privilege, and power are worthwhile. They need, in short, a culture.

I would like to conclude this book by assessing three critical values—narrative, usefulness, and craftsmanship—that might create a cultural anchor.

Narrative

Cutting-edge institutions, short and erratic in their time frames, deprive people of a sense of *narrative movement*. Which means most simply that events in time connect, experience accumulates. In the past decade I've been impressed by three innovative attempts to create this sense of narrative connection at work.

The first consists of efforts in Britain and the United States to fashion "parallel institutions" which seek to afford workers with the continuity and sustainability missing in short-term, flexible organizations. These efforts focus on rethinking the nature of labor unions. The idea is to make the labor union serve as a kind of employment agency, booking jobs; the union buys pensions and health care for its members; most important, it provides the community missing in the workplace, organizing crèches, discussions, and social events. Secretaries in Boston and communications workers in Britain have tried to establish such parallel institutions.

In so doing, they are challenging as new-fashioned employers sclerotic, traditional unions. The conservative union focused on a particular industry or craft and thus was poorly equipped to keep contact with workers who have to jump from one kind of labor to another; by contrast, a more forward-looking union like the United Auto Workers in America now enrolls young university lecturers in its ranks. Traditional unions put their energies mostly into wages and material conditions; the Boston secretarial union concentrates on the communal needs of women and single parents. Service and seniority were the hallmarks of the old social capitalism, and conservative unions follow that time guide. The parallel union seeks to make a narrative thread of experience, as in its employment agency activities, for people who are not yet gray-haired.

The second way of threading experience together over time lies in job sharing. Here the Dutch have been pioneers. The Netherlands has as much as the United States suffered from outsourcing and the disappearance of labor into the developing world. The Dutch response has been to design a system in which available work is divided up in halves or thirds. The job network system further contains a good deal of open entry, so that a person can labor at more than one part-time job as market conditions permit. The Dutch, by temperament the most self-lacerating of Europeans, have found much wrong with the way job sharing operates, but the principle is accepted, and when practiced, this scheme has provided employers with a tool useful in a volatile economy, society with a tool for social inclusion.

Job sharing offers a special kind of narrative frame. A person is continually in work, long-term. This avoids the light-switch anxiety of short-term contracts—now I'm engaged, now I'm redundant. The self-respect from being in work is maintained, even if one works only part of the week or part of the day. Job sharing has the further advantage of permitting people to sort out family–work relations, particularly child care, on a reasonable and predictable basis.

The third way of shaping time under new conditions can enable people to plan long-term. This policy began as an idea which, glimmering a decade ago in the minds of a few radical academics, is now making its way into the real world.

The radical version, pushed by Claus Offe and Van Pariij, was a "basic income" scheme which would replace the welfare bureaucracies of northern Europe by a simpler system which gives everyone, rich and poor alike, the same basic income support to spend or misspend as the individual wants. All individuals would be able to buy education, health care, and pensions on the open market; further, unemployment benefits would disappear, since everyone has the minimum annual income needed to support themselves. Taxes support everyone at a minimum level of life quality, but the Nanny State disappears; if you misspend your income it's your problem. Moreover, everyone gets this basic income whether they need it or not; means-testing disappears.

As these tonic notions made their way into the real world, the promise of providing people the means for long-term personal planning came to the fore. The radical proposal for basic income modulated into the notion of basic capital, that is, giving each young adult a pot of cash to use on education, on purchasing a house, or as a nest egg for hard times. The American jurist Bruce Ackerman has been pivotal in this shift; the results have appeared in Britain legislation which will provision young people this way, though the pot has been filled by a somewhat abstemious, Scotch-Presbyterian hand.

All three of these efforts address a hard reality: insecurity is not just an unwanted consequence of upheavals in markets; rather, insecurity is programmed into the new institutional model. That is, insecurity does not happen *to* a new-style bureaucracy, it is made to happen. These and kindred efforts aim to countervail against that program without returning to the rigidities of time within the old-style social capitalist organization.

The policies turn on a cultural pivot, which concerns narrative itself. If the well-made plot has gone out of fashion in fiction, it is a rarity in ordinary life; life histories are seldom shapely. In ethnography, we are indeed less concerned with how coherent are the stories people tell us than with the effort of our subjects to make their experience cohere. This is not a one-shot effort. Frequently a subject will retell and reorganize an event, sometimes taking apart a seemingly logical story into disconnected bits, in order to see what lies beneath the surface. In technical lingo, this is "narrative agency," the narrator actively engaging and interpreting experience.

In the new institutions, people can frequently succumb to feeling they have no narrative agency; that is, that they lack the power to interpret what is happening to them. We've seen one concrete reason for this; in new institutions, when intermediate layers of bureaucracy are stripped away, information can remain intact as it passes from center to periphery, with relatively little modulation. People subject to this process frequently complain that they have, as Albert Hirschmann put its, no voice within the institution.

Here are three experiments which give people, culturally, more agency in interpreting their experience in time, long-term. As policies, the experiments are small in scale, but as cultural practices they are largely suggestive.

Usefulness

Feeling useful means contributing something which matters to other people. As the scope of uselessness has expanded in the political economy, it might seem that people could compensate through the more informal relations of civil society. A supposedly over-the-hill, middle-aged computer programmer might, for instance, find useful activity in a community or church organization. This is an approach which follows from Robert Putnam's writings on social capital, in which voluntary participation is the crux. While volunteering is certainly a worthy act, this approach risks reducing usefulness to a hobby.

More consequent values for usefulness appear in two realms: among paid public service workers, the second among people doing unpaid domestic labor.

A few years ago I participated in an interview project which sought out British public service workers, running the gamut from street cleaners to surgeons in the public health service.[1] For a generation—like their American counterparts—they had been under attack, their institutions derided as inefficient, themselves demeaned as people who couldn't make it in the world of private enterprise. Many of the people we spoke to were also self-critical; they knew from within how rigid and risk-averse these public bureaucratic pyramids were. Yet despite the criticism they stayed in public service. Our question was, why?

It fell to me to interview immigrants who change bedpans in run-down public hospitals; they could have made more money in better-run private clinics. The reason these hospital attendants stayed was a matter of status. The purpose of the National Health Service— health care for all—elicits the respect of most Britons; for these immigrants, the institution gave them a positive, institutional place in British society.

Status is perhaps the most elusive word in the sociologist's lexicon. While it is often used as a synonym for snobbery, its deeper value has to do with legitimacy. You have status when institutions confer legitimacy upon you. Being useful falls within this framework;

more than doing good privately, it is a way of being publicly recognized.

Another line of interviews turned up the same sentiment among noncommissioned officers in the army, who stayed rather than work easier hours as private security personnel. Interviewers in yet another branch of the project talked to people higher up the civil service. Though they received more verbally elaborate responses to the question "Why do you stay?" still the verbal meat boiled down to the same bone: more recognition for one's work in the public than in the private realm. Of course there are slackers, particularly in British transport services. Even there we found a good deal of peer pressure exerted on the lazy or time-serving; their frustrated colleagues put a high premium on professionalism, another cognate of status. And while conditions in the Inland Revenue or Home Office could drive any man or woman to drink, these institutions' purpose makes the work matter to the public, and so meaningful to the workers.

Voluntary service is of course a worthy act. Here, though, the State confers status on those who do useful work. In so doing, the state acquires authority. As we've seen, institutions at the cutting edge walk away from issues of authority and legitimacy—issues they can't handle. And for this social reason, a truly progressive politics would, in my view, seek to strengthen the State as an employer, rather than hive-off public service work to private companies.

Once we think positively about the State as a source of legitimate, useful activity, progressive politics could deal with those people performing useful labor in families, mothers caring for children, adults caring for aged parents. In my view, government should pay them. The Putnam view is that people "volunteering" to do love's drudgery represent the ultimate test of social capital. The error in this kind of thinking is to equate domestic usefulness with altruism. Care work may be loving, but the work itself has no public recognition; it is an invisible gift, and many of the men and women who do it feel they have dropped out of the adult society of their peers. Were government to reward care work, people would not labor in that limbo.

As a practical matter, care work of all sorts represents an enormous slice of time and effort in the domestic economy. The economy used to benefit by driving a wedge between paid and unpaid care work. Today, the expansion of old age combined with the desires of many women to have careers outside the house has disrupted that old balance. Both these changes have opened up new opportunities for immigrant labor to do care work. Against these trends, however, is the need of both the elderly and the young to be taken care of, emotionally as well as practically, in ways only family members can provide. A truly progressive politics should make that possible, I believe, for men as well as for women.

If only reformers could accept that usefulness is a public good, they could engage with the anxiety and fear of uselessness spawned by the most dynamic sectors of the modern economy. For the reasons I presented in the second chapter, the cult of meritocracy is unlikely to salve these anxieties; exploring new ways for people to be recognized as useful has to be more inclusive. Usefulness itself is more than a utilitarian exchange. It is a symbolic declaration which matters most when the polity confers it, as it can to even the lowest worker in the public services and as it does not to people in the domestic sphere.

Craftsmanship

The third value which could countervail against the culture of the new capitalism is craftsmanship. It represents the most radical challenge but is the hardest to imagine in terms of policy.

Craftsmanship broadly understood means the desire to do something well for its own sake. All human beings want the satisfaction of doing something well and want to believe in what they do. Yet at work, in education, in politics the new order does not and cannot satisfy this desire. The new work world is too mobile for the desire to do something well for its own sake to root into a person's experience over the course of years or decades. The educational system which trains people for mobile work favors facility at the expense of digging deep. The political reformer, imitating the cutting-edge culture in private institutions, behaves more like a consumer ever in search of the new than like a craftsman proud and possessive of what he has made.

Craftsmanship challenges the idealized self supposed by new work, educational, and political institutions. This is a self adept at change, a master of process. At its origins, psychologists like Abraham Maslow celebrated this ideal of self as responsive, open to experience, capable of growth, a self of potential powers. This idealized self indeed has real obvious strengths, and the craftsman's realm is in certain ways smaller and more guarded. Worrying about getting something right mobilizes obsessive elements of the self; getting something right can then lead to a kind of ungenerous possessiveness. Competition is no stranger to craftsmanship, and good craftsmen, be they computer programmers, musicians, or carpenters, can be highly intolerant of those who are incompetent or simply not as good.

For all this, craftsmanship has a cardinal virtue missing in the new culture's idealized worker, student, or citizen. It is commitment. It's not simply that the obsessed, competitive craftsman may be committed to doing something well, but more that he or she believes in its objective value. A person can use the words *correct* and *right* in describing how well something is done only if he or she believes in an objective standard outside his or her own desires, indeed outside the sphere of rewards from others. Getting something right, even though it may get you nothing, is the spirit of true craftsmanship. And only that kind of disinterested

commitment—or so I believe—can lift people up emotionally; otherwise, they succumb in the struggle to
survive.

We've seen why commitment is in increasingly
scarce supply in the new capitalism, in terms of institutional loyalty. The sentiment would be irrational—
how can you commit to an institution which is not committed to you? Commitment is equally difficult in the
new culture's recipe for talent. Mental mobility eschews getting deeply involved; ability is focused on operational technique, as in the SAT, an exercise in problem solving rather than problem finding. Which means
that a person becomes disengaged with the reality beyond his or her own control.

Commitment poses a more profound question
about the self-as-process. Commitment entails closure,
forgoing possibilities for the sake of concentrating on
one thing. You might miss out. The emerging culture
puts enormous pressure on individuals not to miss out.
Instead of closure, the culture counsels surrender—
cutting ties in order to be free, particularly the ties bred
in time.

What I have sought to explore in these pages is
thus a paradox: a new order of power gained through

an ever more superficial culture. Since people can anchor themselves in life only by trying to do something well for its own sake, the triumph of superficiality at work, in schools, and in politics seems to me fragile. Perhaps, indeed, revolt against this enfeebled culture will constitute our next fresh page.

Notes

Introduction

1. Zygmunt Bauman, *Liquid Modernity* (Cambridge: Polity Press, 2000).

Chapter 1. Bureaucracy

1. Karl Marx and Friedrich Engels, *The Communist Manifesto* (Oxford: Oxford University Press, 1998), 6.

2. Joseph Schumpeter, *Capitalism, Socialism and Democracy* (New York: Harper, 1975), 82–85.

3. Socio-Economic Security Programme, *Economic Security for a Better World* (Geneva: International Labor Organization 2004).

4. Leslie Sklair, *Globalization: Capitalism and Its Alternatives* (Oxford: Oxford University Press, 2002).

5. Max Weber, *Economy and Society* (Berkeley: University of California Press, 1978), 2:1156.

6. Robert H. Wiebe, *The Search for Order* (New York: Hill and Wang, 1967).

7. George Soros, *The Crisis of Global Capitalism: Open Society Endangered* (London: Little, Brown, 1998).

8. Max Weber, *The Protestant Ethic and the Spirit of Capitalism* (London: Routledge, 2001), 123.

9. Richard Sennett, *The Corrosion of Character* (New York: Norton, 1998), 122–30.

10. Richard Sennett, *Respect* (New York: Norton, 2003), 200–204.

11. Saskia Sassen, *The Mobility of Labor and Capital: A Study in International Investment and Labor Flow* (Cambridge: Cambridge University Press, 1998).

12. Robert H. Frank, *The Winner-Take-All-Society: How More and More Americans Compete for Ever Fewer and Bigger Prizes, Encouraging Economic Waste, Income Inequality, and Impoverished Cultural Life* (New York: Free Press, 1995).

13. Georgina Born, *Uncertain Vision: Birt, Dyke and the Reinvention of the BBC* (London: Secker and Warburg, 2004), cf. 212–53.

14. Richard Sennett, *Authority* (New York: Knopf, 1980).

15. Robert D. Putnam, *Bowling Alone: The Collapse and Revival of American Community* (New York: Simon and Schuster, 2000).

16. Harrison C. White, *Markets from Networks: Socioeconomic Models of Production* (Princeton: Princeton University Press, 2002).

17. Sennett, *Corrosion of Character*.

18. Claudio Ciborra, *The Labyrinths of Information* (Oxford: Oxford University Press, 2002), 85–90.

19. Cf. Mark Roe, "The Inevitable Instability of American Corporate Governance," working paper, Harvard Law School, 2004.

20. I owe these corrective insights to my colleagues Judy Wajcman and Robert Howard.

21. Cf. William Julius Wilson, *When Work Disappears* (New York: Knopf, 1996).

22. Sennett, *Corrosion of Character*; Katherine Newman, *No Shame in My Game: The Working Poor in the Inner City* (New York: Knopf, 1999).

23. Michael Laskaway, "Uncommitted: Contemporary Work and the Search for Self: A Qualitative Study of 28–34-Year-Old College-Educated Americans" (Ph.D. diss., New York University, 2004).

Chapter 2. Talent and the Specter of Uselessness

1. Jeremy Rifkin, *The End of Work: The Decline of the Global Labor Force and the Dawn of the Post-Market Era* (New York: Putnam's Sons, 1995); Jeremy Rifkin, "The Return of a Conundrum," *The Guardian*, March 2, 2004.

2. Daniel Bell, *The Coming of Post-Industrial Society: A Venture in Social Forecasting* (New York: Basic Books, 1973); Alain Touraine, *The Post-Industrial Society: Tomorrow's Social History: Classes, Conflicts, and Culture in the Programmed Society* (New York: Random House, 1971).

3. Bonnie Dill, "Across the Boundaries of Race and Class: An Exploration of the Relationship Between Work and Family Among Black Female Domestic Servants (Ph.D. diss., New York University, 1979).

4. Sennett, *Corrosion of Character*.

5. Pierre Bourdieu, *Distinction* (Cambridge: Harvard University Press, 1984).

6. Abraham Maslow, *Motivation and Personality* (New York: Harper and Row, 1987).

7. Martha Nussbaum and Amartya Sen, *The Quality of Life* (Oxford: Oxford University Press, 1993).

8. Richard Lewontin, *The Genetic Basis of Evolutionary Change* (New York: Columbia University Press, 1973).

9. Nicholas Lemann, *The Big Test: The Secret History of the American Meritocracy* (New York: Farrar, Straus and Giroux, 1999).

10. Thomas Jefferson to John Adams, in Lester Cappon, ed., *The Adams-Jefferson Letters* (Chapel Hill: University of North Carolina Press, 1988).

11. Murray Brumberg and Julius Liebb, *Hot Words for the SAT* (New York: Barron's Press, 1989), 75.

12. Bauman, *Liquid Modernity*.

13. Cf., for example, Michel Foucault, *Discipline and Punish* (New York: Pantheon, 1992).

14. Michael Young, *The Rise of the Meritocracy* (New Brunswick: Transaction Publishers, 1993).

Chapter 3. Consuming Politics

1. Robert Reich, "The Revolt of the Anxious Class," speech given to the Democratic Leadership Council, November 22, 1994, 3.

2. Simon Head, "Inside the Leviathan," *New York Review of Books*, December 16, 2004, 80.

3. Cf. McKinsey Global Institute, "US Productivity Grown, 1995–2000," Section VI, "Retail Trade," online at www.mckinsey.com/knowledge/mgi/productivity.

4. Cf. Liza Featherstone, *Selling Women Short* (New York: Basic Books, 2004).

5. Albert O. Hirschman, *The Passion and the Interests: Political Arguments for Capitalism Before Its Triumph* (Princeton: Princeton University Press, 1977).

6. Vance Packard, *The Hidden Persuaders*, (New York: D. McKay, 1957).

7. Vance Packard, *The Waste-Makers*, (New York: D. McKay, 1960).

8. Sharon Zukin, *Point of Purchase* (London: Routledge, 2004), 185.

9. Ibid.

10. Guy Debord, *Society of the Spectacle* (Detroit: Black and Red, 1977).

11. Erving Goffman, *Gender Advertisement* (New York: Harper and Row, 1976).

12. Frances Yates, *Theater of the World* (Chicago: Chicago University Press, 1969).

13. Michael Bull, *Sounding Out the City: Personal Stereos and the Management of Everyday Life* (Oxford: Berg, 2000).

14. Cf. the passages on the agora as a modern of democracy scattered throughout Hannah Arendt, *The Human Condition* (Chicago: University of Chicago Press, 1998).

15. Hannah Arendt, *Willing* (New York: Harcourt Brace Jovanovich, 1978).

16. Ulrich Beck, *Risk Society* (London: Sage Publications, 1992).

17. Sennett, *The Guardian*, March 20, 2001.

18. Samuel Huntington, *Who Are We? The Challenges to America's National Identity* (New York: Free Press, 2004).

19. Seeley Brown, *The Social Life of Information* (Boston: Harvard Business School Press, 2000).

20. Polly Toynbee and David Walker, *Better or Worse? Has Labour Delivered?* (London: Bloomsbury, 2005).

Chapter 4: Social Capitalism in Our Time

1. "The Common Good," *The Guardian*, March 20, 2001.

Index